Solomon Says

Godly Counsel for Victorious Living

Cheryl Doss Gangl

Published by KHARIS PUBLISHING, imprint of KHARIS MEDIA LLC.

All KHARIS PUBLISHING products are available at special quantity discounts for bulk purchase for sales promotions, premiums, fund-raising, and educational needs. For details, write:

Kharis Media LLC
709 SW Elmside Drive
Bentonville, AR 72712

Tel: 1-479-599-8657
info@kharispublishing.com
www.kharispublishing.com

ACKNOWLEDGMENTS

I am grateful to the Lord for giving me this opportunity to share His words with others to encourage them to be the best they can be as they travel along the path of life. I am also thankful for my husband, Bert, who listened to me as I put this study together and graciously helped edit this book and the material in my blog. Those times of reading and studying together were so special. I also want to thank my daughter, Caroline, for giving her mommy time to work on her book and for being a willing example for some of my stories. I appreciate the team at Kharis, especially Francis Umesiri and Mercedes Walker, for giving me a chance to publish this study, and I'm thankful for my dear friend DeAnna Gass for helping in the final proof stages. And, lastly, I would like to extend my heartfelt gratitude to all the dear ladies who believed in me and helped me to test this study before it was published. You are an amazing group of women, and I learned so much from you.

Endorsements for *Solomon Says* by Cheryl Gangl

Solomon Says: Godly Counsel for Victorious Living by Cheryl Gangl presents an extremely helpful study for believers who desire to be fully devoted followers of Christ. Cheryl's engaging style is punctuated by insightful and current life applications thoroughly grounded in biblical truth. In addition to the basic study format which is well paced and balanced, the Leader Guide provides worthy suggestions for those who seek to disciple fellow believers by sincere investment in their lives.

Each of the 10 lessons could stand alone as a worthy independent study. Taken together, the chapters form a beautiful tapestry of wisdom teaching which can benefit the new believer and the time seasoned Christian as well. Even though the overall length of each study could be considered brief, any person who follows this curriculum will be extremely well rewarded. After a lifetime of biblical study and 49 years of gospel ministry I can wholeheartedly recommend this special study of Proverbs to any and all who have embarked upon the joyful journey of life in Jesus Christ our Lord and Savior.

Edwin Jenkins, D.Min, Founding Director, LifeLift Ministries, Athens, Alabama

Cheryl Gangl's study on the wisdom in Proverbs is a guide I plan to work through annually. She presents 10 aspects of life that can quickly and easily hinder our ability to honor God if left unchecked. Continually evaluating these areas is an important discipline of the Christian life and Cheryl walks us through Scripture, stories and personal assessments in a simple and easy-to-follow format. The book would work for both group and individual studies and is a valuable resource to share with others we encounter on our journey.

Jennifer Davis Rash, Editor-elect, The Alabama Baptist newspaper

Cheryl Gangl has written an excellent resource for the church. This thoughtful, engaging, and interactive guide will be beneficial for either small group study or personal devotion use. More than simply a study on Solomon's words in Proverbs, Cheryl uses the whole counsel of the Bible to help the reader identify key characteristics that define a grace-changed heart and thus give the believer tools and tips to help cultivate and bear in their lives some of the God-honoring fruit and attributes that we find in Proverbs. Her questions and exercises will provoke the reader to inspect their personal weak areas, leading to her Bible-rich remedies that will help to re-calibrate the heart of faith. This is a great study - I can't wait to use it in church!

John Lemons, Minister to Young Adults, First Baptist Church of Huntsville, Alabama

In over 25 years of ministry, I have never seen a Bible study that is both so practical and rich in the Word at the same time. The *Solomon Says* Bible study is soaked in both Scripture and scriptural stories and is written in a way that immediately allows you to put its principles into practice. I have been best friends with Cheryl Gangl since 1990. I can assure you, you are learning from a teacher who has exhibited life-long integrity and daily lays her life down to be a servant of Christ. The *Solomon Says* Bible study is for everyone who desires to live a wise, godly life!

Tracie Robbins, Women's Ministry Speaker/Teacher and Dallas Seminary graduate

It is an honor for me to recommend *Solomon Says*. Cheryl presents a captivating look at Proverbs as she covers its overarching themes in this ten-week study. I have always been impressed with Cheryl's ability to teach, write, and organize biblical material in an understanding way. You will be thrilled and challenged as you unlock the treasure of Godly Counsel for Victorious Living.

Terry Slay, Adult Education Minister, Mount Zion Baptist Church, Huntsville, Alabama

I love the way God uses author Cheryl Gangl to encourage others through her passionate studying and writing. Her study of Proverbs reminds readers of the significance of taking time to be reconnected and renewed through God's word. The author's work embodies the hidden treasures of Proverbs. As she leads you on an intimate journey throughout the Scriptures, may you embrace your revelations and then share the tangible treasures for victorious living.

Shannon Talley, Author, Hear My Voice and Committing Suicide to Live Again, VoiceVessel Inspirations, LLC

Starting with the introduction, Cheryl Gangl creates an eager anticipation for us to dig into the Proverbs and be counted among the wise.

I love how Cheryl has taken 10 overarching themes from Proverbs, incorporated related Scripture passages to expound on God's truth, and enabled us to recognize wise and foolish behavior.

Solomon Says is truly Godly counsel for victorious living.

Deree Tarwater, Women's Ministry Director, Whitesburg Baptist Church, Huntsville, Alabama

ABOUT THE AUTHOR

Cheryl Gangl is passionate about helping others find their true value in Christ. She has directed, taught and participated in women's Bible studies for more than 25 years and enjoyed teaching the Bible to students of all ages, from preschoolers to senior adults, during that time. She has also worked as a marketing and public relations professional and college English professor. Since becoming a stay-at-home mom, Cheryl's activities have included volunteer work with various civic, church and school organizations. While her articles have been published in various medical, church and hospitality industry publications, *Solomon Says* is her first book.

At home in Madison, Alabama, Cheryl enjoys traveling with her husband Bert and daughter Caroline; listening to music, especially her daughter singing; reading mystery novels; writing devotions for her blog site; and visiting with friends over lunch.

CONTENTS

Introduction

"The fear of the LORD is the beginning of knowledge, but fools despise wisdom and instruction" (Prov. 1:7).

Have you ever felt foolish? Let's face it, most of us have if we've been on this earth for any length of time. Life brings all kinds of circumstances our way. Sometimes, our choices are clear cut, and, at other times, they are not clear at all. Each of us has to make decisions every day – from mundane choices such as what to eat and what to wear to others that are not so mundane such as what major to choose, whether or not to change jobs, whom to marry, how to discipline our children, or how to care for an aging parent. The list of decisions is endless, and the advice we have access to for these choices is just as endless. A scan of the local bookstore shelves or a quick Google search will testify to that.

> **Fear the Lord**
> *"And now, Israel, what does the Lord your God ask of you but to fear the Lord your God, to walk in obedience to him, to love him, to serve the Lord your God with all your heart and with all your soul, and to observe the Lord's commands and decrees that I am giving you today for your own good?"*
> ***(Deut. 10:12-13).***

As Christians, we know our standard for living is found in the Bible, but even Christians sometimes do not know where or how to find the wisdom they seek in God's Word. Granted, God can speak to us in a variety of ways – through other people, including pastors, Bible study teachers, or friends; through song lyrics; through prayer and fasting; even through actual road signs and license plates as one lady in a Bible study I attended pointed out. But, our key method for gaining godly wisdom is through the fear of the LORD, as Proverbs 1:7 tells us.

What does it mean to "fear the LORD?" In the Biblical sense, fear is a reverence or respect for God. It does not mean we shudder before Him or cower in terror. Rather, it means we know our place before a holy God and realize His greatness – His majesty, power, justice, and compassion. And, there's no better way to catch a glimpse of God and His glory than through the reading of His Word, which enables us to discover the guidelines He lays out before us so that we, too, may gain the wisdom that enables us to live lives that honor Him.

I have to be honest, writing a Bible study on wisdom, considering my own shortfall in that area, seemed a daunting task until I realized that all God was asking me to do was settle in, study His Word, and let Him do the talking. After all, reading the Bible is a conversation with God. So, here we go.

Background

The book of Proverbs is traditionally thought of as a book filled with wisdom. In the Biblical canon, it is grouped together with Job, Psalms, Ecclesiastes, and Song of Songs as one of the Wisdom and Poetry Books. The Hebrew word for wisdom, *chokmah* (Strong's H2451), carries with it both the ideas of artistry and skill in a given craft (Exodus 35:35) and the idea of living in a way that pleases God (Job 28:28).[1] In fact, the words *wise* and *wisdom* are found more than one hundred times in Proverbs. Wisdom is so much more than knowledge. While knowledge pertains to that which is known or learned, wisdom is gained by putting what you have learned and know to be right into practice. Warren Wiersbe defines Biblical wisdom as "looking at the world through the grid of God's truth."[2]

A quick glance at Proverbs reveals its poetry as well. The book is filled with a variety of short statements, many of which compare two seemingly unrelated things. And, in many places, it jumps from topic to topic with each line. Wiersbe describes this pattern as being "more like a kaleidoscope than a stained glass window: we never know what the next pattern will be."[3] I believe this unique pattern is what makes this book beautiful and useful. Hebrew poetry is known for conciseness; the idea of a whole lesson can be conveyed in one sentence. Solomon uses epigrams – pithy, witty, and paradoxical sayings – throughout the book of Proverbs.

Because these sayings are isolated in the book, a student of Proverbs should look at what all the Proverbs say on a topic and what the whole Bible says to get the complete picture. Proverbs Commentator Bruce Waltke notes, "It is a single component of truth that must fit together with other elements of truth in order to approximate the more comprehensive, confused pattern of real life.... To avoid overstating truth or teaching half-truths through isolated proverbs, sages call on their disciples to learn all of them."[4] That is how we will study this book. Many have suggested that people study Proverbs as a daily reading because there are thirty-one chapters in the book, which fits nicely into one month of reading. In this study, however, rather than reading consecutively through Proverbs, we will study several overarching themes found throughout the book, taking one topic each week for ten weeks. These ten themes will provide wisdom for living a godly life. The topics found in each of the chapters are not always easy to do, but, if we apply them to our lives, they will help us avoid the pit that sin drops us into and help us rise out of the pits we have already fallen into.

So, who wrote the sage advice of Proverbs that we will be studying? The primary author is Solomon, as noted in the first line of the book. However, Chapter 25 begins a section by "the men of Hezekiah," a group of scholars who lived during the time of King Hezekiah. They are attributed with compiling chapters 25-29, while Chapters 30 and 31 are attributed to "Agur, the son of Jakeh" and "King Lemuel." Some scholars believe Lemuel is another name for Solomon.[5] Scholars have found that many of the sayings in Proverbs are similar to sayings found in ancient Egyptian and Asian manuscripts. However, the difference between these ancient texts and Proverbs is God's inspiration of the sayings found in Proverbs. According to Waltke, "Proverbs mixes seemingly mundane sayings that may have originated outside of Israel with distinctively theological sayings pertaining to the LORD to give a holistic view and a theological interpretation of wisdom peculiar to Israel."

Finally, in Proverbs 22:17, Solomon attributes some of his writings to "the wise."[6]

The primary author of Proverbs, Solomon, is known as the wisest king because, when God told him to ask for a blessing, he asked for wisdom (1 Kings 3:9). Who could be a better source of instruction? 1 Kings 4:32 tells us, "He spoke three thousand proverbs and his songs numbered a thousand and five." As you work through this study, consider Proverbs 2:1-5: "My son, if you accept my words and store up my commands within you, turning your ear to wisdom and applying your heart to understanding – indeed, if you call out for insight and cry aloud for understanding, and if you look for it as for silver and search for it as for hidden treasure, then you will understand the fear of the LORD and find the knowledge of God."

Ask God for wisdom as you read each chapter in this study. My prayer for you is that He will answer you as He did Solomon in 1 Kings 3:12: "I will give you what you asked for! I will give you a wise and understanding heart such as no one else has had or ever will have!" (NLT) So, let's treasure hunt God's Word together in order to live victoriously and grow closer to Him.

The Holy Spirit

This study focuses on pursuing a victorious life, but it is important to note that victorious living is only achieved with the help of the Holy Spirit. Just as a tree needs water, food and sunlight to grow, each of us needs the Holy Spirit to guide and strengthen us as we seek to honor the Lord through godly living. In Romans 8, Paul reminds us that, in our sin nature, we do the things we hate (8:14-15); however, we overcome this through our life in Christ because "the Spirit helps us in our weakness" (8:26). As you focus on each chapter, seek God's wisdom as you pray through each area of your life and allow His Holy Spirit to guide you into truth and provide the strength and grace you need to be transformed to be more and more like Christ. The Lord longs for us to seek him, and as you work through this study, I pray you grow closer to him and live victoriously.

---

1. "H2451 - chokmah - Strong's Hebrew Lexicon (KJV)." Blue Letter Bible. Accessed 27 Jun, 2018. https://www.blueletterbible.org//lang/lexicon/lexicon.cfm?Strongs=H2451&t=KJV
2. Warren W. Wiersbe, *Be Skillful: God's Guidebook to Wise Living*, OT *Commentary Proverbs* (Colorado Springs, CO: David C Cook, 1995), 17.
3. Ibid., 22.
4. Bruce K. Waltke, *The Book of Proverbs Chapters 1-15*. *The New International Commentary on the Old Testament* (Grand Rapids, MI: William B. Eerdmans Publishing Company, 2004), 38-39.
5. Wiersbe, *Be Skillful*, 18-19.
6. Waltke, *Book of Proverbs 1-15*, 66.

1   Humility

"Humility is the fear of the LORD; its wages are riches and honor and life"
(Prov. 22:4).

It is really no coincidence that humility should be the first theme we look at for living a victorious life. The fear of the LORD begins with humility, knowing our place before a holy God. Passages in Ezekiel, Isaiah, and Revelation reveal fearful and majestic descriptions of God on His throne. In our daily lives, we often lose sight of how holy God is and, in our self-reliance, we try to put ourselves in His place.

Read Isaiah 6:1-7 and Revelation 1:9-18.

What is our place before God?

_____

_____

_____

God is holy and we are so unclean that we cannot even stand before Him. Recognition of this truth is humility. We are made in God's image and He does love us, but we must remember our place before Him. When we understand that everything we have comes from Him, humility can flow through us. When we are humble, we:

- Let go of pride.
- Put others first.
- Don't think of ourselves as better than others.
- Have a Christlike, servant attitude.

The Hebrew word for *humility* in Proverbs 22:4 is *anavah*, meaning gentleness, humility, or meekness (Strong's H6038).[1]

In Philippians 2:3 and 1 Peter 5:5, the Greek word for *humility* is *tapeinophrosynē*, meaning a deep sense of one's (moral) littleness, modesty, humility, or lowliness of mind (Strong's G5012).[2]

With the above Hebrew and Greek translations in mind, read Proverbs 22:4, Philippians 2:3, and 1 Peter 5:5 and write your own definition of humility.

What does humility in action look like?

Throughout the Bible, we see many people who displayed humility by putting aside their own fears and agendas in order to follow God.

> "Do nothing out of selfish ambition or vain conceit. Rather, in humility value others above yourselves,"
> (Phil. 2:3).
>
> "Clothe yourselves with humility toward one another, because, 'God opposes the proud but shows favor to the humble'"
> (1 Pet. 5:5).

How did each of the following show humility?

Moses (Exodus 3:5-6)

_____

_____

_____

Hosea (Hosea 1:2, 3:1-5)

_____

_____

_____

Esther (Esther 4:16)

_____

_____

_____

Jesus (Philippians 2:5-8 and Mark 10:45)

_____

_____

_____

Humility can be exemplified in a variety of ways. Moses acknowledged the holiness of God by removing the sandals from his feet at the burning bush. Hosea put God's command over his own wishes by marrying an adulterous wife and then buying her back after she proved unfaithful. Esther knew that only God could save her people and instructed them to fast and pray for His protection over their lives. Jesus provides us with the ultimate example of humility: In His divinity, He did not consider Himself equal with God the Father; He came to earth as a man, took on the role of a servant to men, and died on a cross so that others could be reconciled to God and saved from their sin. Even though we are not divine like Jesus, we can still learn from His actions and humility as a man on earth.

Jesus did not judge others. He chose disciples who were not in the top social class (Mat. 4:18, Mark 2:14). He ate with hated tax collectors (Mark 2:15-16). He associated with Samaritans, a class of people the Jews looked down upon (John 4:9). He stood up for a woman caught in adultery, and He allowed a sinful woman to anoint him with oil (John 8:3-7, Luke 7:36-50).

Jesus helped others. On various occasions throughout the Gospels, Jesus healed those with physical ailments ranging from deafness and blindness to lameness. He raised people from the dead (Lazarus and Tabitha) and healed mental illness by casting out demons (Luke 8:26-39, 9:37-43). Ultimately, Jesus provided spiritual healing for all mankind through His death and resurrection (John 3:16)!

Jesus put the needs of others before his own needs. He knew His purpose in life and willingly obeyed His father to fulfill that purpose (Luke 22:42). He traveled from town to town preaching to and healing great multitudes of people. He patiently and calmly answered every question the Pharisees and synagogue leaders presented to Him, even as they tried to trap Him (Mat. 12:9-12, 15:1-9, 16:1-4).

Jesus was forgiving and left justice to the Father. He did not retaliate when He was mocked by family, friends, and enemies. He practiced what he taught about turning the other cheek (Mat. 5:39). Even as He was being crucified, He prayed, "Father, forgive them" (Luke 23:34).

What are ways that you can be humble in your current life situation?

_____

_____

_____

Turning 180 Degrees

The opposite of humility is pride. While humility is covered over and over in the Bible, pride is covered much more.

Read Proverbs 8:13. How does God feel about pride and arrogance?

_____

_____

_____

According to Proverbs 11:2 what are the results of pride? Of humility?

_____

_____

_____

The Lord makes it clear that He hates pride and arrogance, and the result of these is disgrace. Disgrace, lack of favor, can come in many forms, none of which are pleasant.

Match the disgraceful result of pride to the verse.

Destruction/Fall   Proverbs 13:10
Lack of prosperity/Trouble   Proverbs 16:5
Quarrels   Proverbs 16:18-19
Punishment   Proverbs 18:12
Downfall   Proverbs 28:13-14

Describe a prideful time in your life. What were the results?

_____

_____

_____

Haman serves as a perfect case study for pride. Take the time to read Esther. Its ten chapters tell the story of a sovereign God who honors His people, the exiled Israelites, through the actions of Esther and Mordecai, Jewish cousins with humble hearts. While Esther, Mordecai, and the Jewish people are humbly fasting and praying for the LORD to save them, prideful Haman, on the other hand, expects to receive high honor from King Xerxes for his efforts to annihilate the Jews.

Read Esther 6 and 7:10. Describe the results of Haman's pride.

_____

_____

_____

Proverbs 16:18 says, "Pride goeth before destruction, and a haughty spirit before a fall" (KJV).

How true! Haman's story can be ours, too, if we are not careful. What a fall Haman experienced. He had to honor the person he detested in all the ways he himself wanted to be honored. Even worse, he lost his life on the very gallows he prepared for the person he hated the most. Haman was only thinking of his own needs and desires and he became blinded by hate. While we can see how wrong he was, he could not. Pride can rear its ugly head in any number of ways that may seem innocent to us who experience it.

How did the following people exhibit pride, and what was the result?
Joseph (Genesis 37:5-11, 23-28)

_____

_____

_____

King Belshazzar (Daniel 5:22-28, 30)

_____

_____

_____

Peter (Mark 14:27-31, 66-72, John 13:9)

_____

_____

_____

Pride can rear its head when we place undue emphasis on our position in life. Joseph was no doubt thrilled as he told his brothers about the dream God gave him, which showed him placed in a position of authority over them. However, if he had taken the time to consider how this vision from the Lord would make them feel, he probably would have thought twice before sharing his dream with them.

Many of us also tend to take pride in the things we own. Throughout the books of Judges and I and II Kings, kings like Belshazzar "did evil in the sight of the LORD" by glorying in their possessions. Boasting about the things we have and taking credit for gaining them instead of recognizing that all we have comes from the Lord places us in danger of setting ourselves up as gods.

Some of us point to those who fall into sin and tell ourselves that we would never behave as they do. While promises like these may sound noble enough, at their core, they seek to elevate those who make them above others who have fallen. They are, in reality, nothing more than exercises in judgment and pride, both of which God specifically forbids in His word. The apostle Peter learned this lesson the hard way after claiming that he alone would remain faithful to Christ while the other disciples fell away. However, the good news for those of us who fail to live up to our promises as Peter did is that, like him, we can learn from our shortcomings and, with God's forgiveness and strength, go on to lead lives of humility in Christ.

In addition, Peter exhibited pride when he told Jesus to wash all of him instead of letting Jesus serve him by washing his feet. Peter was usurping the role of master when he made this request, and he was acting in false humility when he did not want to be served by his master. Ironically, the very people who have servant's hearts are often the hardest to serve. There is no shame in being served; in fact, accepting the service of another is a beautiful act of humility which blesses the giver.

Do you struggle with pride in your own life? Write a prayer of confession, asking God's forgiveness and laying hold of His promise in 1 John 1:9, which tells us that "If we confess our sins, he is faithful and just and will forgive us our sins and purify us from all unrighteousness."

_____

_____

_____

_____

_____

_____

What *Fuels Your Pride?*
Prayerfully consider what causes pride to erupt in your life.

❖ *Do you feel the need to control everything? Do you doubt God can handle any situation you encounter? See Colossians 1:15-17 and Luke 1:37.*

❖ *Do you claim ownership and credit for the things you have or do you believe that all things belong to God and that He provides us with everything we need? See Psalm 24:1 and James 1:17.*

❖ *Do you tend to compare yourself to others, causing arrogance, jealousy, or anger? See Philippians 2:3-4 and Matthew 7:3-5.*

1. "H6038 - `anavah - Strong's Hebrew Lexicon (KJV)." Blue Letter Bible. Accessed 27 Jun, 2018. https://www.blueletterbible.org//lang/lexicon/lexicon.cfm?Strongs=H6038&t=KJV

2. "G5012 - tapeinophrosynē - Strong's Greek Lexicon (NIV)." Blue Letter Bible. Accessed 27 Jun, 2018. https://www.blueletterbible.org//lang/lexicon/lexicon.cfm?Strongs=G5012&t=NIV

2 Honesty

"The Lord abhors dishonest scales, but accurate weights are his delight"
(Prov. 11:1 NET©).

According to Proverbs 11:1, how does the Lord feel about "dishonest scales"?

_____

_____

Honesty in our dealings with others is vitally important to God. A quick glance at several Bible translations of this verse shows the intensity of the Lord's feelings about dishonesty:

> *detests* (NIV, NLT)
> *abhors* (NET©)
> *hates* (ISV)
> *considers an abomination* (NASB, ESV, KJV)

Proverbs 20:10 repeats this idea as well.

The idea of dishonest scales comes from a practice in which businessmen owned two sets of weights to use in their transactions: a heavier set when they wanted to purchase an item, so that the item would appear to weigh less than it actually did and, thus, cost less, and a lighter set of weights for selling an item, so that the item would appear heavier than its actual weight and, therefore, cost more.

Proverbs 11:1 contrasts a false balance with a just weight. In Hebrew, the word for *false* is *mirmah* (Strong's H4820), meaning fraudulent, deceit, or treachery.[1] The Hebrew translation for *just* is *shalem* (Strong's H8003), meaning whole, perfect, and of full and just number and measure.[2] Proverbs 11:1 includes strong words that should not be taken lightly. Dishonest business practices did not just occur in Solomon's day. They exist today, too.

What are some ways that fraud takes place in our world today?

_____

_____

_____

Fatal Business Dealings in the Bible:

Consider Ananias and Sapphira.

Read Acts 5:1-10. How were Ananias and Sapphira dishonest?

_____

_____

_____

According to verse 4, who did they lie to?

_____

_____

_____

What was the consequence of their lying?

_____

_____

_____

While the Bible is not exactly clear on why Ananias and Sapphira lied, we can surmise that fear or greed may have been their motivation. Regardless of the reason, their story illustrates God's abhorrence of lying and hypocrisy and the devastating consequences of dishonesty.

Dishonest dealings usually boil down to one reason: distrust toward God. Consider what you know about God and then consider what you really believe about Him.

Our actions come as a result of our thoughts and beliefs. That is why it is so important that we guard our hearts; they are the wellspring of life (Prov. 4:23). When you read promises and commands in the Bible, do you really believe them? Consider your answer as you reflect on how you would react in the following situations.

You receive extra pay from a job that does not require a W2 form and is not part of your usual annual income. *Do you report this income and tithe from it?*

"'Bring the whole tithe into the storehouse, that there may be food in my house. Test me in this,' says the LORD Almighty, 'and see if I will not throw open the floodgates of heaven and pour out so much blessing that there will not be room enough to store it'" (Mal. 3:10).

When you don't tithe, you are actually stealing from God. Stealing from the government dishonors God as well, since we are commanded to honor authority in Romans 13:1-7.

The clerk at the register gives you more change than she was supposed to, and you realize the mistake after you've already driven home. *Do you take it back to her?*

"The integrity of the upright guides them,
but the crookedness of the treacherous destroys them" (Prov. 11:3 ESV).

Abraham Lincoln (also known as "Honest Abe"), the 16th President,
lived out this principle when he was a young store clerk in Illinois. If he realized he had shortchanged someone, he immediately closed the store and walked the change to that person, regardless of the distance.

You show up late to work and then take a long lunch. *Do you record this on your time card?*

"Whoever can be trusted with very little can also be trusted with much, and whoever is dishonest with very little will also be dishonest with much. So if you have not been trustworthy in handling worldly wealth, who will trust you with true riches?
And if you have not been trustworthy with someone else's property,
who will give you property of your own?" (Luke 16:10-12).

For some, not recording accurate time may seem like a small thing, but take heed. If you aren't honest with your time card, how can you be trusted in larger things like managing other people's time cards? Honest actions bear witness to the genuineness of our faith.

You are browsing around a store and accidentally break a small item. *Do you leave it on the shelf or take it to the cashier and buy it?*

"So whatever you wish that others would do to you, do also to them, for this is the Law and the Prophets" (Mat. 7:12 ESV).

Remembering the "Golden Rule" can help us do the right thing in situations like this.

Have you been dishonest in business or other dealings with money? If so, why do you think you acted dishonestly?

_____

_____

What steps can you take to make up for your dishonest actions?

_____

_____

Honesty Is Rewarded With Trust and Blessing

Read 2 Kings 12:6-16. *What does verse 15 indicate about the handling of the temple money?*

_____

_____

Read Deuteronomy 25:15. *What is the reward for using accurate weights and measures?*

_____

_____

Just as the workers in the temple handled their jobs with integrity and were thus entrusted with handling the temple money without supervision, we, too, find the blessings of respect, trust, and favor from others when we are honest in our jobs and responsibilities. The Lord promises "long life in the land he has given them" to people who are trustworthy. These dual blessings are symbolic of a fruitful life. The land mentioned in Deuteronomy 25:15 refers to Canaan, which was thought to be a delightful place. Who wouldn't want to live a long life in a delightful place?

While honesty in our actions is important, so is honesty in our speech. The Hebrew word for *lie* is *kazab*, meaning falsehood, lying, or anything that deceives (Hebrew Strong's 3577).[3]

According to John 8:44, where do lies come from?

_____

_____

There are many types of lies, ranging from white lies to malicious lies. Someone may lie:

- to avoid hurting someone's feelings: "This dinner was great."
- to save someone from danger (hiding a friend from an abusive spouse)
- to hide their sin or avoid punishment: "I didn't eat that cookie you told me I couldn't have."
- to make themselves feel better by comparison (exaggeration or partial truth about someone else to make yourself look better)
- to hurt another person (slanderous statements)

Have you ever told a lie for any of the above reasons? Which one?

_____

_____

Do you believe you were right or justified in telling those lies?

_____

_____

_____

Because lying in our culture is viewed on a variety of levels from innocent to serious, it is hard for people to believe that all lying is condemned. God makes it clear that He hates lying.

Read Proverbs 6:16-20. How many things does the Lord see as an abomination? Of those, how many relate to lying?

_____

_____

_____

This verse clearly states that the Lord not only does not like but actually strongly hates seven things, and, of those seven, two of them (almost one-third of the list) are related to dishonesty.

However, serious questions arise when telling a lie would actually work for someone else's greater good. For instance, in the book of Joshua, we read that Rahab lied to save the Israelite spies, and she was rewarded for it (see Joshua 2). How do we reconcile a dangerous situation like this with God's hatred of lying? An excellent view on this can be found at gotquestions.org:

> "In an evil world, and in a desperate situation, it may be the right thing to commit a lesser evil, lying, in order to prevent a greater evil. However, it must be noted that such instances are extremely rare. It is highly likely that the vast majority of people in human history have never faced a situation in which lying was the right thing to do."[4]

Usually, the number one motivation for lying is fear: either fear of letting others see our weaknesses or fear of punishment. Before you tell a lie, think about your motivation for telling it. If your reason for telling that lie is anything other than another person's greater good, reconsider whether or not you should tell it.

Match the ways people may lie with the verses below:

2 Samuel 11 (David and Uriah and Bathsheba)   to save someone from danger
Joshua 2:1-7 (Rahab)   to get what you want
1 Kings 21:1-16 (Jezebel)   to hide sin or avoid trouble

People can lie to themselves as well. This is called self-deception (1 John 1:8). Satan is the father of lies (John 8:44), and one of his greatest weapons is deception, which includes self-deception. Even so, 2 Corinthians 2:11 promises that, as believers, we will be able to see through any scheme the devil might bring against us. Remember, our battle is not against flesh and blood but takes place in the spiritual realm, so build up and guard your mind with God's holy word as you seek truth and honesty in your thoughts and actions.

> *"If we claim to be without sin, we deceive ourselves and the truth is not in us"*
> *(1 John 1:8).*
>
> *"in order that Satan might not outwit us. For we are not unaware of his schemes"*
> *(2 Cor. 2:11)*

The book of Proverbs is filled with counsel regarding the consequences of dishonesty and the rewards for honesty. *As you read the verses below, choose one that encourages you the most to be honest in your actions or speech and record it below. Commit your verse to memory and meditate on it daily.*

There are consequences of dishonesty. Match the consequence with the verse:

Proverbs 10:9	falls into trouble and does not prosper
Proverbs 11:3	a crushed spirit
Proverbs 15:4	destruction
Proverbs 17:20	angry looks/anger from others
Proverbs 19:5	will be found out
Proverbs 25:23	punishment and captivity

There are rewards for honesty. Match the reward with the verse:

Proverbs 10:9	saves lives
Proverbs 11:3	security
Proverbs 12:22	the Lord's delight
Proverbs 14:25	bringing joy to others
Proverbs 23:16	guidance

My verse on honesty:

_____

_____

_____

_____

We earn the trust of others by our honest words and actions. When we prove that we can be trusted, God is honored, others are blessed, and we reap wonderful rewards such as security and joy from the Lord.

Commit to being honest with yourself, others, and God.

1. "H4820 - mirmah - Strong's Hebrew Lexicon (NIV)." Blue Letter Bible. Accessed 27 Jun, 2018. https://www.blueletterbible.org//lang/lexicon/lexicon.cfm?Strongs=H4820&t=NIV

2. "H8003 - shalem - Strong's Hebrew Lexicon (NIV)." Blue Letter Bible. Accessed 27 Jun, 2018. https://www.blueletterbible.org//lang/lexicon/lexicon.cfm?Strongs=H8003&t=NIV

3. "H3577 - kazab - Strong's Hebrew Lexicon (NIV)." Blue Letter Bible. Accessed 27 Jun, 2018. https://www.blueletterbible.org//lang/lexicon/lexicon.cfm?Strongs=H3577&t=NIV

4. "Is It Ever Right to Lie?" Got Questions Ministries, accessed September 25, 2016, [http://www.gotquestions.org/right-to-lie.html]

3 Heart Attitudes

"A happy heart makes the face cheerful, but heartache crushes the spirit" (Prov. 15:13).

What does it mean to have a happy heart? A quick glance at this verse in several Bible translations shows that the word *happy* in the verse above can also be translated as glad, cheerful, or merry.

Happiness is a state of mind or an attitude, and God tells us over and over how important it is for us to have the right attitude. So, what attitudes would help us to have a happy heart?

Let's start with positive and negative attitudes.

Do you see life as a cup half full or half empty? Consider this past week. What attitudes did you display?

What's your attitude today?
Joyful
Angry
Thankful
Patient
Forgiving
Jealous
Vengeful
Loving
Bitter
Judgmental
Optimistic
Pessimistic

_____

_____

_____

Look at your list. Which of those attitudes do you think come from a happy heart?

_____

_____

_____

According to the *Oxford English Dictionary*, the heart is defined as the center of a person's thoughts and emotions, especially love or compassion.[1]

The Hebrew word for *heart* in Proverbs 15:13 is *leb* (Strong's H3820), meaning the inner man, mind, will, or heart.[2] The equivalent Greek word is *kardia* (Strong's G2588), which, in the literal sense, means the physical heart that pumps blood through the body and, in the figurative sense, signifies our thoughts and feelings.[3]

From these definitions, we can glean that our beliefs, thoughts, words, attitudes, and actions all originate within our hearts.

Match the following verses to what they tell us about the heart:

Matthew 13:19   the dwelling place of Christ
2 Corinthians 9:7   where love comes from
Ephesians 3:17   where God's Word is sown
1 Timothy 1:5   where generosity begins

Isn't it beautiful to think that our hearts are where God's Word is sown and that, where God's Word is sown, there is hope? Whatever weeds of discontent may have begun to grow in your heart, they can be uprooted by and replaced with God's truth. When this occurs, your heart, the dwelling place of Christ, can grow love, generosity, and other attitudes that bring peace.

In Proverbs 4:23, God tells us that our hearts are of utmost importance: "Above all else, guard your heart, for everything you do flows from it." In other words, our hearts control our life, not only physically because they pump blood throughout our body but also spiritually because they are the seat of our emotions and attitudes; as such, our hearts set the course for our lives.

If you think of your heart as the center of your thoughts and emotions, what are some practical ways you can guard your heart?

_____

_____

_____

Happy hearts bring great benefits to our lives. *According to Proverbs 14:30, what is one benefit of a happy heart?*

_____

_____

_____

The heart at peace brings joy and life to its owner and exhibits kindness and mercy to others, unlike the envious heart, which brings "death." The sinister thing about envy is that it originates in the heart, poisons the heart, and hurts the owner more than its object of wrath. Just as a fungal disease can rot a piece of wood from the inside out, so envy poisons the body from the inside out (rots the bones). In this sense, "bones" is a synecdoche for "body" (synecdoche meaning a part representing the whole).

Consider the term Shakespeare used in his play *Othello*: "jealousy is a green-eyed monster." (3.3.179-80)[4] Why a monster? Why the color green? Jealousy is a monster that attacks and feeds on anything. It will even attack itself. Green is the color associated with sickness because an ill person's pallor can be greenish. The sickness of jealousy or envy can turn a person into a "monster," and this results in self-destruction! Don't let envy settle in and rot your bones.

"The light of the eyes rejoices the heart, and good news refreshes the bones" (Prov. 15:30 ESV). This verse illustrates the effect a happy heart can have on a person's face, which in turn can positively affect the people who see that joyful face.

According to Proverbs 15:30, what is a joyful person's effect on others?

_____

_____

_____

They bring joy and refreshment. The phrase "light of the eyes" signifies the righteousness and joy that a happy heart brings to both its owner and to those who see it. Good health is implied in the second part of the verse in which "bone" is, again, a synecdoche for "body." This good health connotes abundance and full satisfaction.[5]

Read Proverbs 17:22 and fill in the blank:

"A cheerful heart is _____ but a crushed spirit

_____.

Almost all Bible translations of this verse say, "good medicine." For everyone who has ever been sick, it is safe to say that they wanted and appreciated good medicine that restored them. While a happy heart may not cure physical illness, it can help a person through difficult times by uplifting their spirit and giving them a positive perspective on their life and circumstances. Proverbs 18:14 tells us that "A man's spirit will endure sickness, but a crushed spirit who can bear?" (ESV).

Spiritually speaking, a happy heart helps promote the wellness of our souls. Waltke notes, "The difference between exhilaration and depression depends more on a person's spiritual resources than on his circumstances."[6] Your spiritual beliefs have a significant effect upon how well your soul is, especially during difficult times.

What characterizes a soul that is well? See the chart on page 20. Categorize the attitudes by checking "Well" or "Unwell" for each one. Read the verses below and match them to the corresponding attitude in the chart.

James 3:16	*Luke 6:37-42*
James 1:19-20	*James 1:2-4*
1 Thessalonians 5:18	*Psalm 119:165*
Isaiah 40:31	*Psalm 37:7-9*
Matthew 6:15	

Attitude	Well	Unwell	Verse
Envious			
Judgmental			
Peaceful			
Patient			
Angry			
Joyful			
Unmerciful			
Hopeful			
Thankful			

Which of the "unwell" attitudes above do you struggle with most?

"We demolish arguments and every pretension that sets itself up against the knowledge of God, and we take captive every thought to make it obedient to Christ"
　　　　(2 Cor. 10:5).

"Search me, God, and know my heart; test me and know my anxious thoughts. See if there is any offensive way in me, and lead me in the way everlasting"
　　　　(Ps. 139:23-24).

If left unchecked, an unwell heart can become:

- a deceitful heart producing flattery and lies (Psalm 12:2)
- a hard heart leading to trouble (Proverbs 28:14)
- a proud heart producing sin (Proverbs 21:4)
- an unbelieving heart turning away from God (Hebrews 3:12)
- an unclean heart falling into iniquity (Psalm 51:10)[7]

The good news is that there is hope to overcome our negative attitudes and avoid the consequences that they create. Find Bible verses that explain the consequences of the attitude you struggle with and the rewards associated with overcoming it. Meditate on those verses. Read them several times a day. Memorize them. Pray them. Let them really sink in. The second you begin to indulge a thought that propels the negative attitude, stop that thought and replace it with the Bible verse you've memorized that addresses that attitude. We must take every thought captive as 2 Corinthians 10:5 tells us. As David did in Psalm 139:23-24, ask the Lord to search your heart and point out any ways that are offensive to Him. Confess these unhealthy attitudes and ask God for His help to overcome them.

Are there any "well" attitudes in the list just mentioned that you need to cultivate in your heart? Which ones?

_____

_____

_____

List three verses that address those attitudes and will motivate you to adopt them in your life:

1. _____

2. _____

3. _____

Write a prayer saying one of those verses back to God.

_____

_____

_____

It's easy to have a happy heart when things are going well for us. But, when we are offended, suffering, or depressed, the task becomes much harder. Even so, the benefits are well worth the effort. Don't wait until life gets hard to begin the practice of thinking Biblically. Find the verses that mean the most to you and your struggles now and write them out, pray them, sing them, memorize them, and etch them on your heart.

1. *English Oxford Living Dictionaries*, s.v. "heart," accessed July 6, 2016, http://en.oxforddictionaries.com/definition/heart
2. "H3820 - leb - Strong's Hebrew Lexicon (NIV)." Blue Letter Bible. Accessed 27 Jun, 2018. https://www.blueletterbible.org//lang/lexicon/lexicon.cfm?Strongs=H3820&t=NIV
3. "G2588 - kardia - Strong's Greek Lexicon (NIV)." Blue Letter Bible. Accessed 27 Jun, 2018. https://www.blueletterbible.org//lang/lexicon/lexicon.cfm?Strongs=G2588&t=NIV
4. William Shakespeare, *Othello*, ed. David Bevington (New York: Bantam Books, 1980), 179-80.
5. Bruce K. Waltke, *The Book of Proverbs Chapters 15-31. The New International Commentary on the Old Testament* (Grand Rapids, MI: William B. Eerdmans Publishing Company, 2005), 6-7.
6. Ibid., 61.
7. Warren W. Wiersbe, *Be Skillful: God's Guidebook to Wise Living, OT Commentary Proverbs* (Colorado Springs, CO: David C Cook, 1995), 53.

4 Generosity

"Do not withhold good from those who deserve it when it is in your power to help them. If you can help your neighbor now, don't say, 'Come back tomorrow, and then I'll help you'" (Prov. 3:27-28 NLT).

"And do not forget to do good and to share with others, for with such sacrifices God is pleased"
(Heb. 13:16).

"Command them to do good, to be rich in good deeds, and to be generous and willing to share"
(1 Tim. 6:18).

"John answered, 'Anyone who has two shirts should share with the one who has none, and anyone who has food should do the same'"
(Luke 3:11).

Freely giving to others is one of the few things in life that is a sacrifice and a joy at the same time. When we give up something of value that we could have kept for ourselves and experience the gratitude and joy it bestows upon another person, we can only feel that same joy ourselves.

In our culture, however, the prevailing thought seems to be to get all you can and keep it. It's yours, and you need lots of stuff! LOTS of stuff! Children feel that way about their toys – any parent who has cleaned a child's room knows this all too well when they begin making the give-away pile. Likewise, a quick glance at social media offers a parade of people showing their vacation pictures, new technology, new outfits, and even their dinner! We are a materialistic culture. But, as adults, we need to strive toward managing our resources in a generous way rather than keeping everything for ourselves. In fact, Christ commands us to be generous.

Read Hebrews 13:16, 1 Timothy 6:18, and Luke 3:11. What is the prevailing theme of these three verses?

_____

_____

Sharing with and giving to others is good and pleasing to God.

Read the following verses, and record the benefits of generosity:

Proverbs 11:25

_____

_____

Proverbs 19:17

_____

_____

Proverbs 22:9

_____

_____

Proverbs 28:27

_____

_____

Generosity reaps refreshment, blessing, fulfilment, and reward from the Lord. Proverbs 11:25 tells us that the generous person will be "prosperous." According to Waltke, this reference does not solely refer to financial prosperity but, instead, should be considered in terms of "wealth, abundance, full satisfaction and health." [1]

Read Proverbs 11:24 and 28:22 and write the consequence of stinginess.

_____

_____

_____

What does Proverbs 23:4-5 say about the longevity of riches? Compare this to Matthew 6:19-21.

> "Do not wear yourself out to get rich; do not trust your own cleverness. Cast but a glance at riches, and they are gone, for they will surely sprout wings and fly off to the sky like an eagle"
> (Prov. 23:4-5).

_____

_____

_____

When a person gains his or her wealth in an unjust way or chooses not to bless others with that wealth, he or she will eventually suffer poverty as their hoarded riches waste away. It is a fact of life that material items will not last forever; they can be taken away and they will deteriorate eventually. Spiritually speaking, people who hold on too tightly to a possession become "owned" by that possession, and they will waste away on the inside because they miss out on the joy that comes from helping others. Stingy people miss

> "Do not store up for yourselves treasures on earth, where moth and rust destroy, and where thieves break in and steal. But store up for yourselves treasures in heaven, where neither moth nor rust destroys, and where thieves do not break in and steal; for where your treasure is, there your heart will be also"
> (Mat. 6:19-21 NASB).

out on friendships as well. Regardless of the form, poverty, whether it be physical or spiritual, will eventually come upon the stingy person.

Generosity in Forms Other Than Material Possessions

We can be generous with more than just our material possessions. We can also be generous with our time. More often than not, love is spelled t-i-m-e. This idea of investing quality time with others is vital and is one of those "treasures in heaven" that cannot be taken away…ever. Consider a favorite material gift you have received from someone and compare it to a favorite time you spent with that person. Which one holds more value in your eyes?

Which is easier to give: money/material items or time? If you answered money/material items you are in the majority. It is much easier to write a check or swipe a credit card than it is to set aside an hour to visit someone you haven't seen in a while or participate in an unplanned activity.

Our lives are so filled with activity that any time we have left over is usually spent sleeping or simply doing nothing. Make a point to step back and invest time in people around you. Arrange your schedule so you can spend time with an elderly neighbor, a single mom, a volunteer-run ministry, or even your family.

According to James 4:13-15, what are we guaranteed time-wise?

> "Now listen, you who say, 'Today or tomorrow we will go to this or that city, spend a year there, carry on business and make money.' Why, you do not even know what will happen tomorrow. What is your life? You are a mist that appears for a little while and then vanishes. Instead, you ought to say, 'If it is the Lord's will, we will live and do this or that'"
> (James 4:13-15).

_____

_____

_____

We are not guaranteed anything, not even the number of our days, so we should make the most of our time. To live a life without regret, invest your time in others for the glory of God.

Lastly, we can be generous with our emotions, lavishing grace and compassion upon those who need them. At times, it can be easier to get angry than to forgive, but God commands us to forgive others just as He has forgiven us (Matthew 6:12). While there are times when righteous anger is justified, consider each situation in your life and ask yourself whether the situation or the person is more important to you. If it is the person, generously extend compassion and grace to the people in your life.

What does Colossians 3:12 say we should do with compassion?

_____

_____

Depending on your translation, this verse tells us to either "put on" or "clothe" ourselves with compassion. The Greek word used here is *endyō*, which means to sink into a garment (Strong's G1746).[2] When we put on compassion, we are immersing ourselves in it, draping ourselves with it. Compassion becomes a part of both our inner being and outward appearance – a part of who we are.

Read the following passages and note the types of generosity shown (possessions, time or compassion):

Dorcas (Acts 9:36-39)

_____

_____

Barnabas (Acts 4:36-37)

_____

_____

Philip (Acts 8:26-40)

_____

_____

Ruth (Ruth 1:16)

_____

_____

The Good Samaritan (Luke 10:30-35)

_____

_____

Dorcas was generous with her possessions and time as she lovingly made clothes for the people in her community. Barnabas was generous with his possessions as he gave money to the church. Phillip had compassion on the Ethiopian and set aside time to help him understand the Scriptures. Ruth lavished love on her mother-in-law by vowing to remain with her, even if that meant walking away from her own hometown and everything familiar to her. And, did you notice the Good Samaritan showed all three types of generosity? He had enough compassion to stop and help a man in trouble, and he used his resources to take care of him. The Good Samaritan did not worry about how much time it would take; he was generous with everything he had.

All of these examples translate to modern day life as well. We can generously provide for people in need, we can support local churches and charities, we can tell others about Jesus, we can be loyal to family and friends, and we can stop to help those in trouble.

Think of some examples where you have shown or have been shown generosity. *As you list your examples, note whether these acts of generosity relate to time, compassion, or possessions.*

_____

_____

_____

Romans 12:9-21 also describes the life of a person who is generous with possessions, time, and compassion.

Read the following verses and mark the types of generosity you find: time, possessions, or compassion. *Choose one of these aspects of generosity in your life that you would like to grow and meditate on the verses you marked that illustrate that type of generosity.*

Romans 12:9-21

Love must be sincere. Hate what is evil; _____

cling to what is good. _____

Be devoted to one another in love. _____

Honor one another above yourselves. _____

Never be lacking in zeal, but keep your spiritual fervor, _____

serving the Lord. Be joyful in hope, patient in affliction, _____

faithful in prayer. Share with the Lord's people who are in need. _____

Practice hospitality. Bless those who persecute you; _____

bless and do not curse. Rejoice with those who rejoice; _____

mourn with those who mourn. Live in harmony with one another. _____

Do not be proud, but be willing to associate _____

with people of low position. _____

Do not be conceited. Do not repay anyone evil for evil. _____

Be careful to do what is right in the eyes of everyone. _____

If it is possible, as far as it depends on you, _____

live at peace with everyone. Do not take revenge, my dear friends, _____

but leave room for God's wrath, for it is written: _____

"It is mine to avenge; I will repay," says the Lord. _____

On the contrary: "If your enemy is hungry, feed him; _____

if he is thirsty, give him something to drink. _____

In doing this, you will heap burning coals on his head." _____

Do not be overcome by evil, but overcome evil with good. _____

Which type of generosity is the hardest for you to give: time, possessions, or compassion?

_____

_____

_____

Which type of generosity would you like to grow in your life?

_____

_____

_____

Write a prayer for guidance in how you can be more generous in the aspect you listed above.

_____

_____

_____

1.   Bruce K. Waltke, *The Book of Proverbs Chapters 1-15. The New International Commentary on the Old Testament* (Grand Rapids, MI: William B. Eerdmans Publishing Company, 2004), 507.

2.   "G1746 - endyō - Strong's Greek Lexicon (NIV)." Blue Letter Bible. Accessed 27 Jun, 2018. https://www.blueletterbible.org//lang/lexicon/lexicon.cfm?Strongs=G1746&t=NIV

5 Time Management

"A little sleep, a little slumber, a little folding of the hands to rest – and poverty will come on you like a thief and scarcity like an armed man" (Prov. 6:10-11).

Some people just never seem to have enough time: not enough time to finish all the tasks set in a day, not enough time to meet a deadline, not enough time for sleep, or not enough time to prepare dinner, much less eat it at the dinner table. If you fall into this category, you are not alone. *Busy* is the buzzword of our culture. Why are we so busy? And if we are not "busy," why do we still have trouble finding enough time in a given day to complete our obligations?

> *"Everyone who is called by my name, whom I created for my glory, whom I formed and made" (Isa. 43:7).*

Here are two reasons:

1. Wasted time
2. Overscheduling

According to Isaiah 43:7, the Lord has given us a purpose in life – to glorify him – and how we spend our time should reflect that purpose. This is not to say that you have to pray, sing praise songs, and read your Bible all day long in order to bring glory to God. On the contrary, we glorify God by doing the things that point to Him as the giver of our joy and eternal, abundant life. So, with that in mind, "wasted time" can be defined as time spent on things we are not passionate about, things that take us away from the person God created us to be, or anything that keeps us from doing God's will. Reflecting on this concept, can you think of examples of wasted time in your life?

To get you thinking, I've included an example of each of these from my life:

Wasted time on things I'm not passionate about:	*Volunteering to do something out of obligation or guilt instead of listening to the voice of God*
Wasted time on things that take me away from the person God created me to be:	*watching TV shows that are not edifying*

Wasted time on things that keep me from doing God's will:	*cleaning the house instead of working on writing this study*

In addition to wasting our time, we can overschedule our time, resulting in stress and frustration for both ourselves and everyone around us. It is easy to schedule every minute of our day with errands, visiting friends, meetings, vacations, lessons, sports, concerts, dates, etc. While all of these things by themselves can be good, when you fill your entire day with them, you create stress, which is not good.

Looking at your weekly schedule, do you think you are too busy?

_____

_____

_____

Reflect on the things filling your calendar. *Choose a few of your routine activities and record their purpose (why are you doing them).*

Activity	Purpose

Proverbs includes a multitude of verses that cover the topics of industriousness and laziness. To be industrious is a good thing – God made us for work. In Genesis 2:15, God created man and put him in the garden to tend and care for it. According to Ephesians 2:10, "we are God's handiwork, created in Christ Jesus to do good works."

We were created to work. However, we were not created to work aimlessly, which results in busyness, but to be industrious. Industriousness involves working toward a purpose, but busyness is aimed more at filling up time for the sake of filling it.

If you kept a log of what you did every half-hour for a day or a week, on what would the majority of your time be spent? Are you overscheduled due to busyness? How could you turn your busyness into God-honoring industriousness?

_____

_____

_____

The concept of using our time wisely is mentioned throughout Proverbs.

Read the following verses and note the benefits of using time wisely and the consequences of not using time wisely. Some of the verses may list only a benefit or only a consequence.

Verse	Benefit	Consequence
Proverbs 6:10-11		
Proverbs 10:4-5		
Proverbs 12:11		
Proverbs 12:14		
Proverbs 13:4		
Proverbs 14:23		
Proverbs 18:9		
Proverbs 19:15		
Proverbs 20:4		

Several of the above verses describe the inaction of the sluggard. When we think of a sluggard, we think of a person who is extremely slow and maybe even dull-witted.

Read Proverbs 26:13-16. Commentator Derek Kidner aptly notes, "The sluggard in Proverbs is a figure of tragi-comedy, with his sheer animal laziness (he is more than anchored to his bed: he is hinged to it, 26:14), his preposterous excuses ('there is a lion outside!' 26:13, 22:13) and his final helplessness."[1] While humorous in illustration, these verses become more serious when we recognize ourselves in them.

Can you relate to any of these?

- Making excuses to not start or not finish projects due to irrational fear (v. 13).
- Not doing anything out of your comfort zone (v. 14).
- Being too weary to do work that meets even the most basic of needs (Waltke notes

"weary" refers to mental and spiritual exhaustion).
- Thinking you know better than everyone else (Waltke explains that "seven men" symbolizes perfection, which further emphasizes the irony that the sluggard is truly disillusioned about his "wisdom").[2]

Time is short. Use your time wisely by taking stock of what God has for you to do. Embrace it and honor your commitments. Be available to serve when you are called to do it, but remember that just because you can do something does not mean that you should do it. There is a time and season for everything. Sometimes, we are called to play on the team and, sometimes, we are called to sit on the sidelines. Be sensitive to God's voice in your life regarding where you should be. When you do that, your time will be used wisely.

What do the following verses say about how or why we should use our time wisely?

Psalm 90:12

_____

_____

_____

Ecclesiastes 3:1-8

_____

_____

_____

John 17:4

_____

_____

_____

Ephesians 5:15-16

_____

_____

_____

James 4:14

_____

_____

_____

We use our time wisely to gain wisdom and to bring glory to God. We use our time in season (being sensitive to what we should be or should not be doing) and make the most of every opportunity because our time is short. The reference to "evil days" in Ephesians 5:16 is a reminder that the world will be filled with deceit by false prophets, so we should be prepared. To be prepared, use your time studying and practicing God's Word.

Two Examples of Wise and Unwise Use of Time from the Bible

1. Joseph (Genesis 39-41)

Joseph's time in jail gives us a picture of someone using his time wisely. Because of his good character and the way in which he used his skills, Joseph ended up being placed high in command over Egypt, the country in which he was imprisoned! He never forgot God, and God protected him and received glory through Joseph's diligence and wise use of time.

2. David (2 Samuel 11)

David, a man after God's heart, illustrates an unwise use of time. When he, as a king, should have been with his army, he chose to stay at home instead. David was gazing over the city from his rooftop when he saw Bathsheba, the wife of another man. From this one moment, David found himself in an adulterous affair, resulting in taking another man's wife and also her husband's life.

While the book of Proverbs is filled with the idea of industriousness as opposed to laziness, the Bible does emphasize rest as well. God gives us the ultimate example of rest in Genesis when He rested on the seventh day after He created everything (Genesis 2:2). While God created man to work, He also commands us to rest so that the work we do can be good.

What Does Rest Mean?

Rest does not necessarily mean sitting quietly and doing nothing. Rest can be anything that refreshes you and gives you a break from work. So, whether you like to ride a bicycle, go to the movies, visit with a friend, or take a nap, all of these things can be rest for you.

Do you have times of rest built into your daily routine?

_____

_____

If you answered "no" to this question, how can you adjust your schedule to change the answer to "yes?"

_____

_____

Resolve to use your time wisely by purposefully choosing the activities in which you participate and building in periodic times of rest from those activities.

1. Derek Kidner, *Proverbs: An Introduction and Commentary*. (Leicester and Downers Grove, Ill.: InterVarsity Press, 1964), 42.

2. Bruce K. Waltke, *The Book of Proverbs Chapters 15-31*. *The New International Commentary on the Old Testament* (Grand Rapids, MI: William B. Eerdmans Publishing Company, 2005), 357.

6 Anger

"A fool gives vent to his anger, but a wise man keeps himself under control" *(Prov. 29:11).*

If you've ever been the recipient of another person's anger, witnessed anger between others, or been angry at someone else, you know how damaging anger is to relationships. If you're human, you've felt anger and seen its ramifications. Unchecked anger destroys, and God makes His point especially clear in the book of Proverbs: we should keep our anger in check.

"Anger is the feeling that makes your mouth work faster than your mind."

-Evan Esar, American Humorist (1899 - 1995)

What is anger?

Anger is defined as a strong feeling of annoyance, displeasure, or hostility.[1] The Hebrew translation of the word *anger* most often used in Proverbs is Strong's H639, *aph*, which means nostril, nose, face, or anger.[2] It is interesting that the nose and face are primary images associated with anger. Consider what anger does to a person's face: the lips tighten, the nostrils flare, and the eyes narrow.

Anger is often called a secondary emotion, meaning it is always caused by an underlying primary emotion. Knowing this is key to understanding how to reign in your own anger. **Fear, helplessness, anxiety, insecurity, sadness, embarrassment/humiliation, frustration, hurt, and jealousy are all primary emotions that often result in anger.**

Consider the situations below and choose which of the primary emotions above fits the situation. In some cases, there may be more than one answer:

1. Your child throws a temper tantrum in the grocery store, creating an embarrassing scene. You feel like people are looking at you as if you are the worst parent in the world because you can't control your child.

   _____

2. Your next-door neighbor just bought a brand-new car, the model you've always wanted and have been looking forward to buying in the next few months.

   _____

3. Your significant other hasn't complimented you on your appearance when you obviously spent a long time getting ready in the hopes that you would look "perfect."

4. Your spouse just lost a long battle with cancer.

5. You get lost trying to find a place you've never been before, and there hasn't been a road sign for miles.

Can you relate to any of these situations? Consider the times you became angry this past week. Briefly list the situation along with the underlying primary emotion or other cause that you think led to that anger:

Situation	Underlying Primary Emotion/Cause

Do you see a connection with your anger and a primary emotion? If so, list it here.

Anger is mentioned in several places in the book of Proverbs.
Read the following verses and list an example you have witnessed of the type of anger they describe:

Proverbs 12:16

_____

_____

_____

Proverbs 14:29

_____

_____

_____

Proverbs 15:18

_____

_____

_____

Proverbs 20:3

_____

_____

_____

Proverbs 22:24-25

_____

_____

_____

According to these verses, what are the benefits of keeping anger in check?

_____

_____

Throughout Proverbs, the angry person is described as impatient, quick to jump to conclusions, and quick to give his opinion, which always results in folly and strife. But, the person who keeps his anger in check is described as one who is patient and in control of his emotions, able to overlook an insult and avoid strife because of his understanding.

Snapshots of Anger from the Bible

Genesis 4:1-13

Why was Cain angry? How did his anger affect his actions? What were the consequences of those actions?

_____

_____

_____

1 Kings 21:1-14

What caused Ahab's anger and how did he display his anger? How did Jezebel display her anger? What are the underlying emotions that caused their anger?

_____

_____

_____

Genesis 37:1-36

What was the primary emotion behind the anger of Joseph's brothers? How did they display their resulting anger? What was the final consequence of their anger? (see verses 26, 28, and 34)

_____

_____

_____

Luke 15:11-32

Why was the older brother angry? What was the emotion propelling his anger? Though it isn't clearly written, what do you think was the final result of the older brother's anger?

_____

_____

_____

Jealousy, hypocrisy, greed, pride, and self-righteousness are all underlying emotions that reveal themselves through anger. Cain, jealous and insecure because his brother's offering was honored more than his own, reacted in murderous anger. Hebrews 11:4 explains Cain's lack of faith and spiritual hypocrisy: "By faith Abel brought God a better offering than Cain did." Commentator David Guzik explains, "Cain's offering was the effort of dead religion, while Abel's offering was made in faith, in a desire to worship God in spirit and in truth."[3]

Ahab, greedy for more land, pouted in his anger when he could not have that land, which in turn, motivated his wife Jezebel to follow her own greediness and commit murder. Naboth was murdered because of a dispute over the ownership of a vegetable garden!

Joseph's brothers, jealous and hurt by their younger brother's condescending attitude and the fact that he was obviously their father's favorite son, ultimately sold him into slavery and lied to their father by telling him that Joseph had been killed. This resulted in their father's deep grief over the loss of his favorite son.

And, finally, the prodigal son's brother revealed his own hardened heart and self-righteousness when his destitute brother returned home and their father honored him instead of disciplining or rejecting him. The older brother believed that hard work and honoring his father are the only ways to receive honor himself, and he was insulted that his brother received such royal treatment after behaving so foolishly. Charles Spurgeon explains,

> "The truth here taught is just this: that mercy stretches forth her hand to misery, that grace receives men as sinners, that it deals with demerit, unworthiness and worthlessness; that those who think themselves righteous are not the objects of divine compassion, but the unrighteous, the guilty and the undeserving, are the proper subjects for the infinite mercy of God; in a word, that salvation is not of merit but of grace." [4]

The older brother was not only self-righteous but also harbored bitterness in his heart, most likely over many years. Verse 29 reveals his feelings: "Look! All these years I've been slaving for you and never disobeyed your orders. Yet, you never gave me even a young goat so I could celebrate with my friends." It is clear that he felt that his work was never recognized and that he believed work was required to receive favor and grace. The older brother had everything he needed but did not appreciate it.

Even though anger can certainly be displayed for a multitude of wrong reasons, not all anger is bad. There is righteous anger as well. This is anger that is caused by the wrongdoing of another, specifically something that breaks one of God's laws. A good example of this is John 2:13-17, where Jesus clears the temple. Read those verses and explain the underlying reason for Jesus' anger.

How did he display his anger? Did he use demeaning language? Was anyone harmed?

_____

_____

_____

A close reading of this passage shows that Jesus cleared the temple first by driving out the animals – cattle, sheep and doves (verse 15). He then scattered the money that had been collected that day, and He overturned the sellers' tables. He did not drive out the people with His whip. There is no evidence of Jesus inflicting physical harm on anyone. His language is stern and meant to correct a wrong. The sellers are told not to turn the temple into a sales market. In addition, they were cheating people by charging exorbitant prices for sacrificial animals. In the parallel passage in Matthew 21:12-13, Jesus tells the sellers they have turned His father's house into a "den of robbers."

Another example of righteous anger is found in Exodus 32:19-20, when Moses finds the Israelites worshipping a golden calf instead of God. *Explain why his anger is righteous. Did he display his anger in a righteous way? Why or Why not?*

_____

_____

_____

Moses' anger was righteous because it is aroused out of sadness that the people had disobeyed God by creating and worshipping an idol instead of their Creator. They had turned their backs on God. It is fitting that Moses broke the Ten Commandments since this act is symbolic of the peoples' disobedience in breaking the first two commandments. Moses' second angry reaction was to pulverize the golden calf, sprinkle it in water, and then make the Israelites drink it. While this seems harsh and we know that Moses struggled with impulsive anger (he killed an Egyptian in Exodus 2:11-12 and he struck a rock instead of speaking to it in Numbers 20:10-11), Guzik provides several good reasons why Moses forced the Israelites to drink the calf-powdered water:

- To show that the so-called god was nothing and could be destroyed easily.
- To completely obliterate this idol.
- To give the people an immediate consequence for their sin.
- To make the gold of the idol absolutely unusable, being corrupted with bodily waste.[5]

Even if we have righteous anger, what we do with that anger is still vitally important. It is normal to feel some anger, but it is wrong to inflict it on others in unrighteous ways. Yelling, using demeaning language, causing physical harm, or getting revenge are inappropriate ways to deal with anger. If anger is used in these ways, relationships will be destroyed.

Righteous anger is appropriately displayed when it is:

> *"My dear brothers and sisters, take note of this: Everyone should be quick to listen, slow to speak and slow to become angry, because human anger does not produce the righteousness that God desires"*
> *(James 1:19-20).*

1. Slowly provoked:
God is slow to anger, and He commands us to be slow to anger in James 1:19-20. In 2 Peter 3:9, we are reminded that God is patient and that He does not want anyone to perish. We should express our anger in the same way as our Creator does, patiently and not in a knee-jerk, explosive way.

2. Displayed in a way that honors the law:

God set laws for us in the Ten Commandments (Exodus 20:1-17), and Jesus teaches us about godly living throughout the Sermon on the Mount (Mat. 5-7). If our displays of anger violate any of these laws, it is not righteous. Philippians 1:27a is a good reminder that our actions are a witness to others.

3. Kept under control:

> *"Whatever happens, conduct yourselves in a manner worthy of the gospel of Christ"*
> *(Phil. 1:27a).*
>
> *"In your anger do not sin: Do not let the sun go down while you are still angry, and do not give the devil a foothold"*
> *(Eph. 4:26-27).*

Throughout the Bible and particularly in the Old Testament, we see that God's anger is always under control. His patience prevails and He is purposeful in the administration of discipline through His anger. Psalm 78:38 is one example of this. Paul exhorts the Ephesians to manage their anger purposefully in Ephesians 4:26-27. Turning the other cheek, so to speak, is another aspect of keeping anger under control. Jesus taught this in the Sermon on the Mount (Mat. 5:38-40), and Solomon reminds us of this in Proverbs 12:16. Revenge is never part of righteous anger. Romans 12:14, 16-21 explains that it is the Lord's place, and not ours, to take revenge.

4. Not done to give pleasure:

God created people for His pleasure, and being angry with their actions certainly gave Him no pleasure. If we are to be like our Creator, then our anger should give us no pleasure either. Paul reminds us in Philippians 2:3 that we are to "do nothing out of selfish ambition or vain conceit, but in humility consider others better than yourselves." We are all God's children, and if we practice seeing others in this light, we can keep our anger under control and use it for good rather than evil.

Look back at the situations you listed as moments of anger earlier this week. Do any of them fall into the category of righteous anger? Based on the four characteristics listed above, did you display your anger righteously?

———————————————————————————————

———————————————————————————————

———————————————————————————————

If you have committed unrighteous anger, confess it and write a prayer asking God for help in working through it.

———————————————————————————————

———————————————————————————————

———————————————————————————————

We all display our anger. While some anger is just, not all anger is beneficial, so examining the reasons for your anger will help you manage it if it is unrighteous. Work through root emotions like jealousy and bitterness that cause your anger, resolve to purify your heart from all things that create unrighteous anger in your life, and consider how to display your anger in ways that honor God.

1. *English Oxford Living Dictionaries*, s.v. "anger," accessed July 6, 2016, http://www.oxforddictionaries.com/us/definition/american_english/anger.

2. "H639 - 'aph - Strong's Hebrew Lexicon (NIV)." Blue Letter Bible. Accessed 27 Jun, 2018. https://www.blueletterbible.org//lang/lexicon/lexicon.cfm?Strongs=H639&t=NIV

3. "Genesis 4-Cain and Abel," Enduring Word: David Guzik's Bible Commentary, accessed March 12, 2018, https://enduringword.com/bible-commentary/genesis-4/.

4. Charles Spurgeon quoted in "Luke 15- The Joy of Finding the Lost," Enduring Word: David Guzik's Bible Commentary, accessed March 12, 2018, https://enduringword.com/bible-commentary/luke-15/.

5. "Exodus 32- The Golden Calf," Enduring Word: David Guzik's Bible Commentary, accessed March 12, 2018, https://enduringword.com/bible-commentary/exodus-32.

7 Godly Speech

"Those who guard their lips preserve their lives, but those who speak rashly will come to ruin" (Prov. 13:3).

Have you ever regretted saying something? There seems to be a direct line between what we think and what we say. What's on our mind is usually what comes right out of our mouth.

Why is it so hard not to blurt out our feelings or air our opinions? Our words begin with our attitude toward God, others, and ourselves. If we work toward fearing God as Proverbs 1:7 instructs us, remembering our place before Him, and remembering that Christ died for all sinners, then we have a chance at controlling our tongues when it comes to airing our opinions.

Words matter – they can tear down or they can build up. The old adage "Sticks and stones may break my bones, but words will never hurt me" is a lie. Words can pierce to our very heart, as God reminds us over and over in Proverbs.

What does Solomon say about negative words? Note what they produce and how they are described:

Proverbs 12:6

_____

_____

Proverbs 12:18

_____

_____

Proverbs 14:3

_____

_____

Proverbs 15:4

_____

_____

Proverbs 16:28

_____

_____

Proverbs 18:7

_____

_____

Proverbs 25:23

_____

_____

Proverbs 26:28

_____

_____

Negative words produce great hurt – did you notice the harsh descriptions? Negative words cause death (figuratively), they wound others as if by the sword or a rod to the back, they crush, they separate close friends, they cause complete undoing, they bring angry looks, and they cause ruin.

Wiersbe notes some of the manifestations of evil speech:

> **Negative Self-Talk**
>
> *What do you think about all day? Do you criticize yourself, never giving yourself any grace? If so, heed this warning: What you think about becomes who you are. Proverbs 23:7 tells us "For as he thinks within himself, so he is" (NASB).*
>
> *So, put an end to those negative thoughts and replace them with the truths God says about you. You are a chosen people, you are more than conquerors, you are dearly loved, and you are His.*
>
> *Worrying about what others think about you is another form of destructive internal speech. Proverbs 26:2 encourages us that the truth will prevail and a lie will not endure: "Like a fluttering sparrow or a darting swallow, an undeserved curse does not come to rest." What a great encouragement it is to know that lies and slander are not permanent in the eyes of the Lord.*

Lying – Without truth, there is nothing upon which we can rely. Proverbs 12:22 encourages us to tell the truth. The Lord delights in truth.

Gossip – Reporting personal or sensational facts about others creates division and deeply hurts the person who is being gossiped about. Proverbs 11:13 is a good reminder that we should be faithful friends. Likewise, Proverbs 20:19 encourages us to avoid people who talk too much because, if they freely share their own personal information and that of others, they will also be free with your information.

> "The LORD detests lying lips, but he delights in people who are trustworthy"
>
> (Prov. 12:22).

> "A gossip betrays a confidence; so avoid anyone who talks too much"
>
> (Prov. 20:19).

> "Enemies disguise themselves with their lips, but in their hearts they harbor deceit. Though their speech is charming, do not believe them"
>
> (Prov. 26:24-25).

> "The heart of the righteous weighs its answers, but the mouth of the wicked gushes evil"
>
> (Prov. 15:28).

> "Too much talk leads to sin. Be sensible and keep your mouth shut"
>
> (Prov. 10:19 NLT).

Flattery – Using insincere praise to get what you want only reveals your selfishness and makes you dishonest and manipulative (Proverbs 26:24-25).

Impetuous Speech – Hasty comments, rash promises, and knee-jerk reactions can result in words we regret. Think before you speak! Display a heart of righteousness as described in Proverbs 15:28.

Talking Too Much – Like the adage "Loose lips sink ships," which refers to guarding information from enemy spies (first seen in 1942 on World War II posters), too many words can bring regret. Proverbs 10:19 reminds us that using a little restraint to determine what we say is wise. [1]

What does Solomon say about positive words? Note their results and how they are described:

Proverbs 10:11

_____

_____

Proverbs 10:20-21

_____

_____

Proverbs 10:31-32

_____

_____

Proverbs 12:6

_____

_____

Proverbs 12:14

_____

_____

Proverbs 14:3

_____

_____

Proverbs 15:4

_____

_____

Proverbs 15:23

_____

_____

Proverbs 16:24

_____

_____

Proverbs 25:11

_____

_____

Using positive words brings life, nourishment, wisdom, good things, rescue, protection, healing, and joy. The vivid imagery of positive words includes some beautiful images:

Fountain of life. This picture is a reminder of youth, health, and refreshment.

Choice silver. The image of choice silver, a precious metal, conveys the idea of great worth or something that brings credit to its owner.

> *"A good tongue is healing to wounded consciences, by comforting them; to sin-sick souls by convincing them; and it reconciles parties at variance."*
>
> *-Matthew Henry, English Minister and Bible Commentator (1662-1714)*

Fruit. In Matthew 7:16, Jesus taught that people will be known by their fruit. Do you want your words to represent you as good or evil?

Tree of life. This phrase is an allusion to the tree of life in Paradise, and it conveys the idea that those who eat from it will have life. Waltke notes, "The metaphor is a tree of life whets the appetite to restore Paradise in a broken world through healing speech that gives eternal life to those who 'eat' it."[2]

Honeycomb. When you consider that honey is sweet and used as a remedy, it is appropriate that pleasing words should be compared to a honeycomb.[3]

Apples of gold in settings of silver. According to Gill's Exposition, the apples are either made of gold or golden in color; the settings of silver most likely refer to a silver basket. This presentation would be beautiful. The adverb "fitly" refers to wheels and carries with it the idea of words that roll in right on time. This image refers "to every word that is with grace, and ministers grace to the hearer, and is for the use of edifying, when time, place, persons, and circumstances, are observed."[4]

What does Solomon say about "holding our tongue?"

Proverbs 10:19

_____

_____

Proverbs 11:13

_____

_____

Proverbs 13:3

_____

_____

Proverbs 17:27-28

_____

_____

Refraining from talking too much makes us wise and trustworthy, protects us, and keeps us even-tempered. David's prayer for wise use of words says it beautifully: "Set a guard over my mouth, LORD; keep watch over the door of my lips" (Psalm 141:3). Resolve to pray this verse daily, especially if you struggle with impulsive or reckless speech.

Your Words Set You on a Journey

We may think that only our feet lead us on a path each day, but our tongues also determine the courses we will take. Our words can lead us down the proverbial good or bad paths, depending on what we say and even on what we think (our own internal speech, which influences the actual words we speak). With this in mind, we should consider our words before we say them and be careful not to allow certain thoughts to permeate our mind.

This idea about our words determining our path is emphasized in two of the three analogies James uses to illustrate the power of the tongue. In James 3, He uses the example of the bit placed in a horse's mouth to enable the rider to control the horse. In the second analogy, the tongue is compared to a ship's rudder, the slightest movement of which can change the entire ship's course. In both cases, something very small can be used to move something very large and, in both cases, the change of course is done with relative ease. When we apply this principle to our speech, it reminds us how easy it is to say something we will regret. Negative words are often remembered forever by those to whom they are spoken.

Proverbs 18:21 warns us that the tongue has the power of life and death. In his commentary on Proverbs, Kidner says that the power of words relating to life and death have two qualities: penetration and spread. Penetration is what words do to a person internally; words affect our attitude, beliefs, and convictions. Spread refers to the distance that words travel among many people's minds. This can either be positive like a fountain of life or it can be negative in the form of gossip.[5]

> "The tongue has the power of life and death, and those who love it will eat its fruit" (Prov. 18:21).

Every place a negative word is spread, it leaves destruction. Proverbs 16:27 appropriately illustrates the dangerous spread of negative words: "A scoundrel plots evil, and his speech is like a scorching fire." Similarly, James 3:5-6 explains that the tongue is like a small spark that sets a whole forest ablaze.

Think of an example where someone's words spread like wildfire. If you cannot think of anything, look on social media!

_____

_____

_____

List a time when someone's words hurt you.

_____

_____

List a time when you said hurtful words to someone.

_____

_____

Pray for God to forgive you for your hurtful words and to help you forgive those who have hurt you with their words. Ephesians 4:29 reminds us that we should use our words to edify others.

> *"Do not let any unwholesome talk come out of your mouths, but only what is helpful for building others up according to their needs, that it may benefit those who listen"*
> (Eph. 4:29).

List a time when someone's words built you up.

_____

_____

_____

List a time when you built someone up with your words.

_____

_____

Have you ever wished you had held your tongue in a situation? James 1:19-20 is a good reminder of the value of listening.

Consider the following Bible characters and how they either spoke wisely or held their tongues. Match each character to the situation:

Esther (Esther 4:15-5:8, 7:3)

Despite being lied about and jailed, held fast to his principles and did not speak against his boss' wife

Joseph (Genesis 39)

Followed the king's orders, speaking what the king requested, and refraining from giving too much information about his conversation with the king to the king's officials

Jeremiah (Jeremiah 38:14-28)

Waited for the right time to tell her husband, the king, about a plot against her people

As important as it is to be wise in your speech, it is even more important to learn to listen. Consider the following:

_____*Do you interrupt others before they finish speaking?*
_____*Are you thinking about what you want to say next while the other person is still talking?*
_____*Do you feel that what you have to say is more important than what the other person says?*

If you answered "yes" to any of the above, begin working on your listening skills. A friend told me she went to see a counselor for help with her own communication skills and one of the questions she was asked to consider before she spoke was this: "Why am I talking?"

Here are a couple of root heart issues to ask yourself about when it comes to your speech:

_____*Do I struggle with pride (thinking you know best)?*
_____*Do I struggle with insecurity (thinking you're not good enough or not as _____ as the other person)?*
_____*Am I afraid of silence (thinking you must fill the space with chatter if the other person is not talking)?*

One of our greatest opportunities to help others with our speech is to understand our faith enough to tell others about it at any time. Meditate on Colossians 4:6 and 1 Peter 3:15.

> "Let your conversation be always full of grace, seasoned with salt so that you may know how to answer everyone"
> (Col. 4:6)

> "But in your hearts revere Christ as Lord. Always be prepared to give an answer to everyone who asks you to give the reason for the hope that you have. But do this with gentleness and respect" (1 Peter 3:15).

Tone

The way we say words is equally as important as the words we say. Tone, the mood you create with your words, is directly related to your attitude when you are speaking. Even if your words are technically "benign," a good part of their meaning is derived from the tone you convey. The receiving party actually feels the tone of the words you speak more than the words themselves. So, if you struggle with saying things in a pleasant tone, search your heart for the attitudes that create that unpleasant tone and ask God to help you root them out.

How would you answer someone who asked you why you believe in Jesus? Write Colossians 4:6 across the top of a sheet of paper and then write your testimony.

If you do not know Jesus as your Lord and Savior and you desire to make him Lord of your life, see page 77. This is the best decision you will ever make!

How to write a testimony

Your testimony should include three main parts:

1. A description of what your life was like before you accepted Christ. What types of things did you struggle with? How did you meet your needs for acceptance, value and purpose?

2. A description of how you came to accept Christ as your Lord and Savior. What were the circumstances of your life at that time: where were you and who helped you understand your need for Christ? This is a good place to include Scripture and the plan of salvation as it was presented to you.

3. A description of what your life is like since you accepted Christ. What actions, thoughts, attitudes, and emotions have changed in your life? A significant change to mention is that you now have forgiveness and eternal life! End with details about your current situation.

As you write your testimony, remember to:

❖ *Write no more than three minutes of speech.*

❖ *Be honest. Don't exaggerate the events in your life.*

❖ *Speak in your own voice and use words that your audience will understand.*

❖ *Be specific in your descriptions; give details that provide a picture for the listener. But, do not include people's full names. A first name will do. The types of details you want to give are those that will help the listener engage in your story and recognize how much you value your faith.*

❖ *Stay focused on what Christ means to you. Avoid adding details that will not point someone back to Christ.*

❖ *Include Scripture that would help someone understand the plan of salvation. The information listed on page 77 can help you get started.*

1. Warren W. Wiersbe, *Be Skillful: God's Guidebook to Wise Living, OT Commentary Proverbs* (Colorado Springs, CO: David C Cook, 1995), 140-143.

2. Bruce K. Waltke, *The Book of Proverbs Chapters 1-15. The New International Commentary on the Old Testament* (Grand Rapids, MI: William B. Eerdmans Publishing Company, 2004), 615.

3. Bruce K. Waltke, *The Book of Proverbs Chapters 15-31. The New International Commentary on the Old Testament* (Grand Rapids, MI: William B. Eerdmans Publishing Company, 2005), 30.

4. "John Gill's Exposition of the Entire Bible: Proverbs 25," Bible Hub, accessed November 11, 2016, http://biblehub.com/commentaries/gill/proverbs/25.htm.

5. Derek Kidner, *Proverbs: An Introduction and Commentary.* (Leicester and Downers Grove, Ill.: InterVarsity Press, 1964), 46-47.

8 Discipline

"My son, do not despise the Lord's discipline and do not resent his rebuke, because the Lord disciplines those he loves, as a father the son he delights in" (Prov. 3:11-12).

Discipline. This word strikes fear in most of us because it is not pleasant to receive and, often, is not pleasant to dole out either. However, God commands that we receive and administer discipline throughout our lives.

The word *discipline* in Proverbs 3:11-12 refers to correction in the sense of one person putting another person who is doing something wrong back on track. This verse shows the role of being a gracious recipient of discipline, and, for parents, being a willing disciplinarian. Regarding the disciplinarian role, however, this does not mean making yourself the judge and jury of others when you are not involved in a situation. In other words, you are not given the privilege to step in and correct others in situations that don't concern you.

Read Proverbs 26:17 and record what the verse says about meddlers.

_____

_____

_____

Interfering in someone else's quarrel is like seizing a dog by the ears – It is needless and dangerous! Just as when a person pulls on a dog's ears the dog is sure to bite, a meddler will certainly find resistance and hostility. Unless you are part of a conflict or God has told you to intervene, you should simply pray for the people involved. But, keep that prayer between you and God because making a prayer request for another person who has not given permission for it can be gossip.

What discipline does mean is that, as a parent, spouse, or friend, we sometimes have to step up and provide correction to those who need it. Again, it is important to administer this correction only as God leads because He is the ultimate judge and administrator of justice. And, before ever confronting a person, pray diligently that you will have the right words to say and that the people you confront will have willing hearts to hear them.

Reasons for Discipline

> "Because the Lord disciplines the one he loves, and he chastens everyone he accepts as his son"
> (Heb. 12:6).

Why does the Lord discipline us according to Hebrews 12:6?

_____

_____

God disciplines us because He loves us. We should rejoice that our Father in heaven cares for us so much that He is not willing to let us wander away. He disciplines us in order to restore us to fellowship with Himself!

Match the following benefits of discipline to the Proverb:

Proverbs 10:17   receives honor

Proverbs 12:1   gains knowledge

Proverbs 13:18   receives prosperity and blessing

Proverbs 15:32   gains understanding

Proverbs 16:20   shows the way to life

Describe a time when you received discipline and found blessing in it. *What blessings did you find?*

_____

_____

_____

There are times when we can be stubborn, not wanting to hear we are wrong, and we reject the discipline we've been given.

What does Proverbs 29:1 say about the person who continually rejects discipline?

_____

_____

_____

Avoid destruction and be encouraged that discipline, while painful, is temporary and reaps an amazing harvest. Read Hebrews 12:5-11.

According to Hebrews 12:11, what is that harvest?

_____

_____

_____

Hebrews 12:5-11 emphasizes the importance of discipline. Note what verse 11 says discipline produces: a harvest of righteousness and peace!

How Do I Know When I Should Confront Someone?

When you are called to administer discipline, it must be for the right reasons. Consider why you feel called to confront a person. Are your motives pure? Do you love this person and not want to see them hurt themselves or others? Or, are your motives impure? Are you jealous or want to put them in their place? Your motive for administering discipline must be the same as the Lord's: to bring the other person back into fellowship with God.

Consider three times you have administered discipline to a friend or family member and complete the chart below:

Situation	Note the Pure Motives (love, care, safety,...)	Note the Impure Motives (jealousy, revenge, pride,...)	Effect on the Relationship (destruction or restoration)

Consider your answers above and note whether your reasons for disciplining others have been restorative or destructive. Write a prayer asking God for wisdom for future situations.

_____

_____

_____

Discipline for Your Children

In our present culture, many households are ruled by the children, which is an unnatural and unbiblical arrangement. God intended for parents to guide their children, not the other way around. Children need boundaries and should receive discipline when they cross those boundaries. Spanking, revoking privileges, and grounding are just a few ways to administer discipline. The key is finding the right type of motivation for your child and being consistent in how you administer that motivation.

Many adults today were disciplined by corporal punishment and turned out fine. I received plenty of spankings, once with a switch from the tree in our front yard, and I can say that I'm good and even thankful for it because it was proof that my parents actually cared what happened to me. After that particular spanking in the front yard, I never stayed out after dark or went into someone's house without letting my parents know where I was (and this began at 6 years old). God commands us to discipline our children.

According to Proverbs 19:18, what is the reward of discipline?

_____

_____

_____

What does Proverbs 13:24 say about the parent who does not discipline his child?

_____

_____

_____

Discipline produces great reward – your child will learn right from wrong, have absolute values and standards to use later in life, and avoid coming to complete ruin. Waltke explains that "Loving parents seek to correct the faults of their children because … their children's lives, favor, protection, healing, dignity, and prosperity are at stake. Unloving parents turn their backs on them and hand them over to death, social ruin, public exposure, calamity, and shameful poverty." However, the blessings from discipline must be rooted in the following assumptions: the home is where values are transmitted, the parents have absolute values, the child commits folly, and the "rod" is needed only if words are not successful in the discipline.[1]

There are many books on discipline. Among my favorites are *Creative Correction* by Lisa Whelchel, *Parenting Is Not for Cowards* by James Dobson, and *Shepherding a Child's Heart* by Tedd Tripp. Discipline is not easy, and I know. I used to look at my little blond-haired, blue-eyed, angelic-faced toddler and think, "How can I spank this precious little girl?" Then, I would hear my husband's words: "If you don't discipline her now, she will break your heart later." With that idea, my mind would run wild with thoughts of what she would be like as an unruly teenager who had never been told "no" or a fatal situation where she didn't obey me and ran out in front of a car. It was thoughts like these that scared me into action. Even more so, I would remember God's words on children and discipline:

Why do children act out?

*Proverbs 22:15 tells me:*_____

_____

_____

_____

What is at stake if I don't discipline?

Proverbs 23:13-14 tells me: _____

_____

_____

_____

What are the future benefits of my discipline?

Proverbs 29:17 tells me: _____

_____

_____

_____

The "foolishness" or "folly" bound up in the heart of a child in Proverbs 22:15 refers to the idea that we are born with sin in our hearts. Until we learn boundaries through correction, this sin will remain.

The "death" referred to in Proverbs 23:13-14 is spiritual, meaning death of the soul. The "rod" can be interpreted as any disciplinary measure. What the verse means is that discipline administered early on, whatever form it takes, may well correct actions that might prevent a child from maturing spiritually and becoming a responsible citizen.

Just as Hebrews 12:11 reminds us that correction results in peace and righteousness, Proverbs 29:17 tells us that discipline brings peace and delight to the parent's soul.

Discipline should be done in love. Proverbs 3:12 explains that a father disciplines the child in whom he delights. Proverbs 4:4 reminds the child that discipline is expressly for extending life because boundaries are set for safety. Proverbs 13:24 emphasizes the fact that discipline is done because of love and, where there is no discipline, there is no love. Wiersbe

> *"Train up a child in the way he should go, Even when he is old he will not depart from it"*
> *(Prov. 22:6 NASB).*

> *"Hear, my son, your father's instruction And do not forsake your mother's teaching; Indeed, they are a graceful wreath to your head And ornaments about your neck"*
> *(Prov. 1:8-9 NASB).*

says, "What a tragedy when children are left to themselves, not knowing where or what the boundaries are and what the consequences of rebellion will be!" Parents should take comfort in Proverbs 22:6 because, if they guide their children with the truths of the Bible, their children will have a firm foundation and will not stray.[2]

Disciplining our children is not easy, and some days are harder than others. But, the benefits far outweigh the difficulties. So, parents, press on and correct your children patiently and lovingly according to God's Word.

The flipside of parents administering discipline is a child's acceptance of discipline.

According to Proverbs 1:8-9, how should children view instruction from their parents?

_____

_____

_____

From this verse, we can glean that children are instructed to obey and value the instruction from both parents; father and mother are listed on equal ground. Their instruction and teaching is symbolized by a graceful wreath worn on one's head and an ornament worn around one's neck. The wreath, similar to the twisted leaves worn by Olympic winners, symbolizes victory and vindication over enemies. The ornament worn around the neck is a metaphor for guidance and protection. From these symbols, we can infer that children should be grateful for their parents' instruction because it adorns their lives with victory and protection.[3]

God disciplines his children just as earthly parents discipline theirs. We are called to graciously receive God's discipline, remembering that it is for our good and not our detriment. When done correctly, discipline is administered in love rather than anger. Anything done in love is good. Throughout the Bible, we see the Lord disciplining his children.

Why did God discipline the Israelites in Hosea 4:1-2?

_____

_____

_____

Can you relate to any of these offenses?

_____

_____

How did God discipline according to Hosea 2:12?

_____

_____

_____

Read Hosea 2:15. What is the purpose of this discipline?

_____

_____

_____

Read Genesis 3. Why did God discipline Adam and Eve? What were the terms of the discipline (vs. 16-19)?

_____

_____

_____

One of the major themes of Hosea is God's faithfulness to his people who were unfaithful. The Israelites were disobedient; they forgot God, cursed, lied, stole, committed adultery, and murdered. Sadly, this list of sins sounds a lot like the actions of today's culture. God, in His mercy and justice, disciplined His people by putting up obstacles against everything they tried to rely upon, all for the purpose of drawing them back to Himself. God disciplined them to lead to their restoration. And, He will discipline us to restore us to Himself as well.

God's people began disobeying Him when Adam and Eve ate from the forbidden tree. Their discipline has affected every generation since then. Life in Paradise changed drastically: people now experience pain and sickness, disharmony, hard work, and, ultimately, death on earth. All of these things remind us of our frailty and are meant to move us to seek God and rely on Him rather than ourselves.

Every generation in history has fallen astray from their Creator, who wants a relationship with His people. This break in the relationship has led to discipline every time. For a clear picture of this sin cycle, read the book of Judges. Over and over, God's children obeyed Him, got comfortable, forgot God, went their own way, were disciplined by God, and, finally, returned to Him. Then, the cycle began again, and it continues today.

We live in a fallen world and, thus, sin is inevitable. However, we have a merciful God. If we repent of our sins and receive discipline graciously, we are kept safe. God is the ultimate and perfect example of a loving disciplinarian.

Discipline in Friendship, the Workplace and Marriage

Discipline is also administered between spouses, friends, and co-workers. Spouses and close friends have to "discipline" each other at some point. This means gently pointing out a fault that is hindering a person's walk with Christ. Again, remember that you are not the judge or jury and that God must clearly tell you to confront a person. As Proverbs 27:17 says, we are to be like "iron sharpening iron," but there is a balance.

My husband and I had to grow into this aspect of our marriage. Early on, I realized that my need for approval from others was only being magnified, rather than resolved, through my marriage. My husband helped me gain confidence and, sometimes, had to point out my faults to get me back on track. While it was very hard to hear, I'm glad he did it because it ultimately helped me see things I was blind to and begin healing through God's word. Any time my husband pointed something out to me, he backed it up with Scripture. This was of utmost importance because it showed me he wasn't picking on me and genuinely had my best interest at heart.

> "As irons sharpens iron, so one person sharpens another" (Prov. 27:17).

Over time, I'm learning to receive this graciously, as God commands. Trust me, at first I wanted to retaliate against my husband; but, when I realized his sincerity and love for me, I understood and appreciated his comments. In these situations, humility is a necessity. Be willing to listen and consider your words before responding. James 1:19 is a must! Make this verse the motto of your life.

Write James 1:19 here:

_____

_____

_____

> "No discipline seems pleasant at the time, but painful. Later on, however, it produces a harvest of righteousness and peace for those who have been trained by it" (Heb. 12:11).

Confronting a friend or employee or receiving discipline from them is difficult as well. Again, if your motives are pure, pray for the right words to say and go forward. It will not be pleasant, as Hebrews 12:11 reminds us; however, healing can take place if both parties are humble. You are not responsible for the other party's reaction, but you are responsible for your own actions.

Two Confrontations in the Bible

Read 2 Samuel 12:1-18.

What did the Lord call Nathan to do?

_____

_____

_____

Describe Nathan's rebuke - what it was and how he did it.

_____

_____

_____

What was David's reaction?

_____

_____

_____

Read Galatians 2:11-16.

Why did Paul oppose Peter?

_____

_____

_____

How did he do it?

_____

_____

_____

In both of the situations above, discipline was required to correct an affront to God. Nathan showed David that he was using people to get what he desired, and Paul corrected Peter's wrongful treatment of Gentile Christians and his works-based actions that had taken the place of faith in Christ. Nathan's rebuke was done privately because it dealt with David's private life. However, Paul publicly corrected Peter because his behavior was done in public and affected all the Christians in the room. Confronting someone for the purpose of correction is not easy, but, if it is done after much prayer and in love with the right motives, the reward is restoration and peace.

1. Bruce K. Waltke, *The Book of Proverbs Chapters 1-15. The New International Commentary on the Old Testament* (Grand Rapids, MI: William B. Eerdmans Publishing Company, 2004), 574.

2. Warren W. Wiersbe, *Be Skillful: God's Guidebook to Wise Living, OT Commentary Proverbs* (Colorado Springs, CO: David C Cook, 1995), 125.

3. Waltke, *Book of Proverbs 1-15*, 187-188.

9 Justice

"Do not say, 'I'll pay you back for this wrong!' Wait for the LORD and he will avenge you" (Prov. 20:22).

We have opportunities every day to remember that justice is the Lord's. And, because we live in a fallen world, we will be hurt by sin, either our own or someone else's. If you are like me, your first reaction is to try to get even or to return evil for evil. But, that is not what God commands.

Consider the following situations. *How would you react? Be gut-level honest:*

You are snubbed by a fellow church member when you see her in the church hallway.

_____

_____

Someone cuts you off in traffic.

_____

_____

A friend betrays your confidence.

_____

_____

Your spouse cheats on you.

_____

_____

A drunk driver kills your child.

_____

_____

It is so easy to seek revenge when someone hurts you, but the Lord says it is not our place to dispense justice. That task belongs to the Lord alone.

Read the following verses from Proverbs and describe why we should leave room for the Lord to give justice:

Proverbs 24:1

_____

_____

Proverbs 25:21-22:

_____

_____

While we often cannot understand why things happen, we can trust that our Father in heaven sees us and that He rewards us for obeying Him. No evil act escapes His notice. Our reward for leaving justice to the Lord is reconciliation with the offending party and, ultimately, peace with God. 1 Peter 3:9 further explains that we will inherit blessings.

Proverbs 25:22 mentions heaping burning coals on your enemy's head. While some may believe this is an active form of punishment, Waltke explains that the image actually relates to shame: "Most commentators agree with Augustine and Jerome that 'coals of fire' refers to the 'burning pangs of shame' that a person will feel when good is returned for evil, his shame producing remorse and contrition."[1] Returning good for evil does not absolve our enemies' guilt for the evil they have done. They will face the consequences of their sinful actions. In addition, leaving justice to the Lord keeps us in a position of obedience to Him. When we respond to evil with evil, we become like the people who offended or wronged us and we disobey God. Proverbs 26:4-5 explains that answering "a fool according to his own folly" makes us like the fool.

> "Do not repay evil with evil or insult with insult. On the contrary, repay evil with blessing, because to this you were called so that you may inherit a blessing"
> (1 Pet. 3:9).

> "Evil will never leave the house of one who pays back evil for good"
> (Prov. 17:13).

Just as God rewards us when we leave justice to Him, Proverbs 17:13 shows us that we will inevitably face consequences when we return evil for good. Sadly, this proverb is one that is "close to home" for Solomon because his parents, David and Bathsheba, lived out the promise in this verse when their unfaithfulness (Bathsheba as a wife, David as a protector and friend) to Uriah resulted in their first child's death.[2]

Read the following verses and record what each of them says about God's sovereignty in your life:

Romans 8:28

_____

_____

Jeremiah 29:11

_____

_____

God can bring good out of a situation, even when all we see is the bad. He can weave things together in ways we cannot fathom. Isaiah 55:8 reminds us that "'my thoughts are not your thoughts, neither are your ways my ways,' declares the LORD." His sovereignty is benevolent – it offers us hope!

Consider the following lessons from the Bible:

Even when Saul was pursuing him relentlessly, David clearly understood that justice belonged to the Lord. Although Saul tried to kill him multiple times and David had many chances to kill Saul, David always refrained from doing so. When Abishai was ready to strike down Saul, David told him, "'Don't destroy him! Who can lay a hand on the LORD's anointed and be guiltless? As surely as the LORD lives,' he said, 'the LORD himself will strike him; or his time will come and he will die, or he will go into battle and perish'" (1 Sam. 26:9-10).

In the New Testament, we see accounts of Jesus living out this principle. Jesus did not try to get even when people spit on Him, called Him names, and betrayed Him. He lived what He taught in the Sermon on the Mount: "Love your enemies and pray for those who persecute you, that you may be children of your Father in heaven" (Mat. 5:44-45). The apostle Paul gives us great advice in Romans 12:9-21, which is one of my favorite passages in the Bible because I believe it is the key to living a life of peace with others.

> ### A Warning About Judging
>
> *If you are tempted to be judge and jury and take justice into your own hands, consider what Jesus says about this:*
>
> *"Do not judge, or you, too, will be judged. For in the same way you judge others, you will be judged, and with the measure you use, it will be measured to you"*
>
> *(Mat. 7:1-2).*

Read Romans 12:9-21. Looking specifically at verses 17-20, list the five commands regarding leaving justice to the Lord:

1. _____

2. _____

3. _____

4. _____

5. _____

In this passage, Paul commands us not to repay evil for evil, to do what is right according to the gospel, to live at peace with everyone, not to take revenge upon others, and to feed our enemies. When we live according to these standards, we leave a legacy of peace and exhibit the light of Christ.

According to verse 21, what is the ultimate result of leaving justice to the Lord?

_____

_____

Consider two times you have been hurt by someone and list those briefly. *What was your reaction? What action did you take? What was the result?*

Situation	Reaction and Action Taken	Result	Did your action align with leaving justice to the Lord?

If you took justice into your own hands in one of the situations you listed, how could you have acted differently? Write the steps you could take to leave justice in the hands of the Lord:

_____

_____

_____

Part of not taking justice into your own hands is the act of forgiveness. *Forgive,* according to the *Oxford English Dictionary,* is defined this way: to stop feeling angry or resentful toward (someone) for an offense, flaw, or mistake.[3] We've all been hurt by someone at some point in our lives, and what we do with that hurt is vitally important. Even if we don't actually lash out at someone to get even, we are still taking justice into our own hands when we do not forgive the other person. We have made ourselves the judge and jury, and that is God's role.

Read Proverbs 10:12 and note what unforgiveness and hatred cause:

_____

_____

_____

> "Hatred stirs up strife, but love covers all offenses" (Prov. 10:12 ESV).

Consider a time when you harbored unforgiveness. What "strife" appeared in your life?

_____

_____

> "Love prospers when a fault is forgiven, but dwelling on it separates close friends" (Prov. 17:9 NLT).

Unforgiveness not only hurts the offending person but it also hurts the one holding onto unforgiveness even more. Unforgiveness can cause bitterness to take deep root in our hearts, and, once that root is there, it is very hard to remove. The more we dwell on angry, unforgiving thoughts, the stronger they become and the more likely we will be to act on them. Unforgiveness causes stress, and stress can create all kinds of health problems.

In addition to health problems, what are the other consequences of unforgiveness described in Proverbs 17:9?

_____

_____

Untold numbers of friendships have been destroyed by unforgiveness. How can we forgive when we are feeling hurt so deeply? I've struggled with this all my life, and, just recently, the Lord reminded me to simply trust Him. Here is good counsel I've been given: pray for the other person until you truly want what is best for him/her, don't withdraw from the other person when he/she offers kindness to you, and wait on the Lord for healing to come. When I realized that we all make mistakes and that God forgave us through the death of His son on the cross, I realized that I should learn to let go of my anger and unforgiveness. After all, how can I withhold forgiveness when I've been forgiven for so much through Christ's death on the cross?

Read Matthew 18:23-35. How does this parable say we are to forgive?

_____

_____

_____

We are to forgive from our heart, not just by offering lip service. Matthew 6:12, which is part of the Lord's prayer, exhorts us to forgive others. When you consider the core message of the Bible, it points to the principle of forgiveness. God created people, they rebelled, they repented, and He forgave and restored them. Jesus died so we could be forgiven. His whole life was about healing, grace and forgiveness. Forgiveness is the key concept of Christianity! Proverbs 19:11 is another good reminder of why we should forgive: forgiveness brings us honor and glorifies God.

> *"Good sense makes one slow to anger, and it is his glory to overlook an offense"*
> *(Prov. 19:11 ESV).*

When we accept Jesus as our Lord and Savior, we find freedom. John 8:32 tells us that the truth will set us free. When we forgive, we are freed from our sin. When we pass on this forgiveness to those who have offended us, we are freed from bitterness and hurt and the offender is freed from our anger. It is important to note that, when we forgive, we are releasing the other person without condoning their sin. When we understand that we are not saying the sin committed against us is okay, we can forgive more easily. We must let the Lord provide the consequences for the other person's sin and not take justice into our own hands. It is also important to note that, if the offender puts you in harm's way, you should not remain in that situation. If necessary, remove yourself from that person's company.

Counselors and any number of websites, articles and books on forgiveness provide different stages of forgiveness but all agree that the deeper the hurt, the longer the process. It is key to understand that forgiveness is a process and not a snap decision. This idea of process implies that you must walk through it and not avoid it or try to get around it.

The wisest counsel I've been given on how to forgive includes three stages. The first stage is seeing the offender as a person again. You begin to remember that he or she is a person with feelings and faults, just like yourself. To even approach this stage, I've prayed for God to give me eyes to see as He does. In addition to seeing things through God's eyes, it also helps to remember our battle is spiritual as Ephesians 6:12 tells us. The devil pits us against each other in so many ways, and it is sad that we often fall into that trap. So, pray for the ability to see your offender as a person like you.

The next stage is deciding you will not return evil for evil. Remember 1 Peter 3:9

and Romans 12:17-21? These verses explicitly command this life principle.

The final stage of forgiveness is being able to pray for good things for the other person. When negative thoughts about the offender or situation creep in, stop them immediately and pray for the Lord to help you. Pray for the offender. While Jesus was being persecuted before his crucifixion, he prayed, "Father, forgive them, for they do not know what they are doing" (Luke 23:34). If Jesus can do that, we can work toward it, too.

Forgiveness is an attitude of the heart, and ultimately it is for our own good. Walking through the forgiveness process heals our hearts, restores our souls and keeps us right with God.

The Lord does understand your hurt because He sees everything. If you are having trouble forgiving someone, commit these promises to your heart:

"The eyes of the Lord are in every place, keeping watch on the evil and the good" (Prov. 15:3 ESV).

"You keep track of all my sorrows. You have collected all my tears in your bottle. You have recorded each one in your book" (Psl. 56:8 NLT).

"Cast all your anxiety on him because he cares for you" (1 Pet. 5:7).

Choose one of the promises above, commit it to your heart, and pray it back to the Lord as you ask Him to help you forgive someone who has offended you.

---

1. Bruce K. Waltke, *The Book of Proverbs Chapters 15-31. The New International Commentary on the Old Testament* (Grand Rapids, MI: William B. Eerdmans Publishing Company, 2005), 331.

2. Ibid., 54.

3. *English Oxford Living Dictionaries*, s.v. "forgive," accessed April 6, 2017, https://en.oxforddictionaries.com/definition/us/forgive.

10 Marriage

This chapter includes two sections: one for married couples and one for singles. Good advice can be gleaned from both sections regardless of your marital status; but, for special emphasis, see the section that applies to you.

For married couples: resolve to be faithful to your spouse.

"Do not let your heart turn to her ways or stray into her paths. Many are the victims she has brought down; her slain are a mighty throng. Her house is a highway to the grave, leading down to the chambers of death" (Prov. 7:25-27).

Chapters 5 through 7 of Proverbs include vivid descriptions of and stern warnings against pursuing the adulteress. The stories in these chapters are not just hypothetical. On the contrary, they describe actual threats to the sanctity and well-being of marriages today. The counsel offered by Solomon is valuable, and we would be wise to heed it.

Forty-one percent. According to a September 2016 research study done by Statistic Brain Research Institute, that's the percentage of marriages in which one or both spouses admitted to committing adultery either physically or emotionally.[1] Startlingly, this number represents close to half of all marriages today. Divorce Statistics Info explains, "A close analysis of infidelity rate and its growth pattern clearly indicates that nearly one half of all married men and women are involved in extramarital affairs. There is something missing in their relationships that compel them to look elsewhere for what they want."[2]

Think about how many times you've heard about an adulterous affair in your own social circles, families, neighborhoods, workplaces, or churches. While adultery seems to be more prevalent now than ever, it is an age-old problem. Solomon addresses this issue with language that is uncompromisingly honest and clear.

Read Proverbs 7.

According to verse 7, who does Solomon see, and how is he described?

_____

_____

_____

What was the young man doing? (verse 8)

_____

_____

_____

Describe the woman who comes out to meet him. (verses 10-13)

_____

_____

_____

Is the woman married? (verses 19-20)

_____

_____

_____

How does she lead the young man astray? (verse 21)

_____

_____

_____

What will his association with the woman cost the young man? (verses 22-23)

_____

_____

_____

What advice does Solomon give to avoid the adulterous woman? (verse 25)

_____

_____

_____

Any of us could easily be the simple-minded youth described in Proverbs 7. Flirting with temptation, whether deliberately or blindly, can quickly land us in a dangerous situation. Kidner succinctly describes the progression of the adulteress' tactics: "First comes shock treatment (13); second a circumstantial story – it is a special day, a celebration; it would be unthinkable to refuse (14). Third, flattery: he is the very one she had to find (15); fourth, sensuous appeal (16-18); fifth, reassurance (19-20). The whole is pressed home with a flood of words."[3]

Men and women, beware of treading toward anyone or anything that puts you alone with the opposite sex. The path to adultery is a subtle one, often beginning with a friendship. When a relationship is built on the sharing of feelings, physical attraction and eventual sin may be quick to follow.

In Proverbs 6:27-29, what is flirting with adultery compared to?

_____

_____

_____

Flirting with adultery is like playing with fire! The warmth may feel good at first, but, when you get too close to it, you will be burned. No amount of concealing or justifying your actions is going to allow you to escape God's judgment or the consequences of your sin.

According to Proverbs 6:26, what is the consequence of adultery?

_____

_____

_____

When you commit adultery, you lose everything from monetary wealth to spiritual and physical well-being. Consider the monetary cost of divorce and alimony, the emotional cost of damaged relationships with your spouse and family, and the monetary and physical costs of contracting a sexually-transmitted disease. Adultery causes loss in all aspects of your life. As Proverbs 6:26 says, you are reduced to a piece of bread, meaning being reduced to extreme poverty.[4] The verse further emphasizes that the adulteress is like a hunter: her purpose is to take your life.

What are other consequences of committing adultery listed in Proverbs 6:31-35?

_____

_____

_____

Saying that the adulteress aims to take your life is an understatement compared to what her husband aims to do to you. According to Proverbs 6:31-35, the adulterer will pay sevenfold, be disgraced, and, ultimately, destroyed. The idea of "sevenfold" signifies "full compensation," which is demanded by the law. However, the jealous husband will not accept any compensation or bribe (35). He will want his day in court, and he will demand the adulterer's life, not his money.[5] The husband will show no mercy (34), and shame will never leave the adulterer (33).

Read Proverbs 5:15-20. What is Solomon's advice to avoid adultery?

_____

_____

_____

Solomon gives sage advice: love your spouse and spend your time and energy on him or her. He instructs us to delight in our spouses through every season of life, from youth until old age. Proverbs 5:15-20 includes images of water streaming privately (in your own well) and publicly in the streets. This is a metaphor for faithfulness (the well) and infidelity (the streets). The imagery is erotic, similar to the language found in Song of Solomon.[6] Further, verses 21-23 bring home the point that infidelity is also an affront against God and that "all man's ways are in full view of the LORD."

Truthaboutdeception.com lists situations that encourage infidelity:

- being too close to or dependent upon someone other than one's spouse
- being around someone who is sexually interested
- spending a significant amount of one-on-one time with someone else
- allowing feelings of distance or disconnectedness toward one's spouse to fester without addressing them
- placing one's self in situations that foster the opportunity for unfaithfulness (e.g., meeting behind closed doors, traveling together for work, etc.)
- engaging in alcohol or drug abuse[7]

Do any of these situations apply to you? If so, end these situations now, ask God for forgiveness, and renew your commitment to your marriage.

In our online world and with more women than ever entering the workforce, romantic connections are much more easily made. Thus, husbands and wives should guard their hearts and marriages by setting boundaries for their other relationships.

My husband and I keep our marriage relationship pure by doing things like not having lunch alone with someone of the opposite sex. We don't keep photos or memorabilia from relationships before we were married. And, most of all, we keep the lines of communication open between us. We go on dates and talk daily by email, text message, and phone when we're apart. We pray together and pray for each other.

With your spouse, list some steps you can take to protect your marriage:

_____

_____

_____

Adultery destroys everything in your life, and its effects are far-reaching, destroying things in the lives of those around you. Avoid adulterous situations at all costs by investing in your marriage and making it your top priority. You may want to see a counselor, attend a marriage conference, or read a marriage self-help book together. Remember to praise your spouse often, dwelling on their good qualities more than the less-than-favorable ones. Spend time just talking to each other. Be gracious. In your Christian walk, you are married to the Lord, and He is faithful to you. Be faithful to Him and, in turn, practice this same faithfulness with your spouse.

For singles: resolve to marry wisely.

"A wife of noble character is her husband's crown, but a disgraceful wife is like decay in his bones" (Prov. 12:4).

The single-most important relationship-related choice you will make, aside from accepting Christ as your savior, is your choice of spouse. Marriage is the most intimate relationship you will ever have with another person. After all, the two partners become one in marriage. So, you should resolve to marry wisely.

The book of Proverbs consists mainly of advice from Solomon to a younger man, possibly a son. Look at the verses below, which refer to the qualities of a wife from two angles: what a man should look for in a wife and how a woman should develop her character to be a suitable partner to a godly man. Of course, the same godly principles required of women should also be required of men (i.e. industrious, peace-loving, etc.).

What qualities in a spouse do the following verses encourage?

Proverbs 19:14:

_____

_____

Proverbs 31:25:

_____

_____

Proverbs 31:26:

_____

_____

Proverbs 31:27:

_____

_____

Proverbs 31:30:

_____

_____

As individuals, we all have preferences about the kind of person we would like to marry such as hair color, height, interests, or education level. While these kinds of traits are good things to desire and the choices are limitless, there are some non-negotiable traits that Christians should look for in a mate: prudence (ability to use good judgment and caution when making decisions), dignity (exhibiting respect and honor for self and others), wisdom, diligence, responsibility, and, most importantly, fear of the Lord.

What qualities do Proverbs 21:9 and 21:19 admonish?

_____

As Christians, we are admonished to avoid those who are ill-tempered or quarrelsome.

Looking at the qualities that are encouraged, which ones are evident in your life? Which ones are missing?

_____

_____

For the ones you listed as missing, choose a verse to meditate upon that speaks about these qualities and write down actions you can take to strengthen these qualities in your life. A few verses on the various qualities from the list above are given on the next page. If the Lord places other verses on your heart, use those as well!

Godly Qualities:

Prudence: Proverbs 19:14

"But test everything; hold fast what is good" (1 Thess. 5:21 ESV).

"When the Spirit of truth comes, he will guide you into all the truth, for he will not speak on his own authority, but whatever he hears he will speak, and he will declare to you the things that are to come" (John 16:13 ESV).

The idea of prudence includes using good judgment and caution before speaking or acting and is paired with wisdom in Proverbs 1:4 and 8:5. A prudent person is wise, and his or her choices reflect this wisdom. Before he would even consider marrying me, my husband prudently requested we listen to a series on marriage. At the time, I was not so sure about the "wisdom" of his idea, but, after we got married, I realized just what a difference working through our issues before marriage made. Our first year of marriage was so much easier than our year of dating because my husband was cautious before making a big decision.

Dignity: Proverbs 31:25

"Whatever happens, conduct yourselves in a manner worthy of the gospel of Christ" (Phil. 1:27a).

"So that you may live a life worthy of the Lord and please him in every way: bearing fruit in every good work, growing in the knowledge of God" (Col. 1:10).

A person with dignity exudes respect for self and others. This person acts honorably. People are complex, so it is wise to get to know someone through all the seasons of a year. The more time you spend with someone talking with them, the better you will get to know them and have insight into their true character. If a potential spouse has undignified traits that you cannot see yourself living with in the future, that person probably will not change those traits after marriage. Seek to be with someone who honors God, himself, and others.

Wisdom: Proverbs 31:26

"The fear of the LORD is the beginning of knowledge, but fools despise wisdom and instruction" (Prov. 1:7).

"But the wisdom that comes from heaven is first of all pure; then peace-loving, considerate, submissive, full of mercy and good fruit, impartial and sincere" (James 3:17).

"If any of you lacks wisdom, you should ask God, who gives generously to all without finding fault, and it will be given to you" (James 1:5).

Wisdom is a major theme of Proverbs, and it encompasses both prudence and judgment. Wisdom does not imply that a person knows everything, but it does mean that the person understands how to handle a given situation based on past experience.

Diligence and Responsibility: Proverbs 31:27

"Whatever you do, work at it with all your heart, as working for the Lord, not for human masters" (Col. 3:23).

"All hard work brings a profit, but mere talk leads only to poverty" (Prov. 14:23).

Throughout Proverbs, the unproductive sluggard is contrasted with his absolute opposite: the diligent and responsible person. The diligent person is industrious. Remember that a person will not change after marriage. If you want to be married to an ambitious person, it is unrealistic to think that the lazy person you are dating will change. Likewise, if the woman does all the leading in dating, she cannot expect her boyfriend to become the leader once they are married.

Fear of the Lord: Proverbs 31:30

"Therefore, my beloved, as you have always obeyed, so now, not only as in my presence but much more in my absence, work out your own salvation with fear and trembling, for it is God who works in you, both to will and to work for his good pleasure"(Phil. 2:12-13 ESV).

"And now, Israel, what does the Lord your God ask of you but to fear the Lord your God, to walk in obedience to him, to love him, to serve the Lord your God with all your heart and with all your soul, and to observe the Lord's commands and decrees that I am giving you today for your own good?" (Deut. 10:12-13).

You and the mate you choose should be "equally yoked" (2 Cor. 6:14). That is, as a believer, you should only consider marrying another Christian. "Missionary Dating" – becoming romantically involved with another person in the hopes of converting them – goes against God's word and, more often than not, will not end well. The more common interests two people have, the better their chances are for a strong marriage. Faith issues run deep, and, if two people do not place a similar priority on spiritual matters, they will have serious problems later.

Ask God for wisdom in your dating life. Be willing to hear what He has to say to you on that subject. After all, His wisdom is limitless while ours is finite. Trust in the infinite wisdom of the Lord and hold on to the promise that He will provide.

Pray the following verse and commit its promise to your heart:

"Commit everything you do to the LORD. Trust him, and he will help you"
(Psalm 37:5 NLT).

1. "Infidelity Statistics - Statistic Brain." 2017 Statistic Brain Institute, publishing as Statistic Brain. September 16, 2016. http://www.statisticbrain.com/infidelity-statistics/.

2. "Latest Infidelity Statistics of USA," Divorce Statistics, accessed September 16, 2016, http://www.divorcestatistics.info/latest-infidelity-statistics-of-usa.html.

3. Derek Kidner, *Proverbs: An Introduction and Commentary* (Leicester and Downers Grove, Ill.: InterVarsity Press, 1964), 75.

4. Warren W. Wiersbe, *Be Skillful: God's Guidebook to Wise Living, OT Commentary Proverbs* (Colorado Springs, CO: David C Cook, 1995), 65.

5. Bruce K. Waltke, *The Book of Proverbs Chapters 1-15. The New International Commentary on the Old Testament* (Grand Rapids, MI: William B. Eerdmans Publishing Company, 2004), 358.

6. Ibid., 319

7. "How Do People Make the Decision to Cheat?" Truth About Deception, accessed September 16, 2016, https://www.truthaboutdeception.com/cheating-and-infidelity/why-people-cheat/decision-to-cheat.html.

Congratulations on completing this study!

My prayer for you is that you have gained Biblical encouragement, strengthened your relationship with the Lord, and been empowered to make the needed changes in your life through prayer and the work of the Holy Spirit. Change is never easy, but, with God, all things are possible (Mark 10:27).

The hard work of introspection, repentance, and living out God's word daily reaps benefits of victory and peace. Continue practicing the godly words of wisdom that Solomon left for us in Proverbs. Don't give up. As the apostle Paul says, "Press on!" You will be glad you did.

I Want to Become a Christian

Living a truly victorious life is only possible when we have a relationship with Christ. We cannot do it on our own. God made us human, and part of that humanness is our propensity to sin, which separates us from God.

"As it is written: 'There is no one righteous, not even one'" (Romans 3:10).

"For all have sinned and fall short of the glory of God" (Romans 3:23).

"For the wages of sin is death" (Romans 6:23a)

But, even though our sin separates us from God, He is still merciful and offers us eternal life through Jesus Christ.

"But God demonstrates his own love for us in this: While we were still sinners, Christ died for us" (Rom. 5:8).

"For God so loved the world that he gave his one and only Son, that whoever believes in him shall not perish but have eternal life" (John 3:16).

"Jesus answered, 'I am the way and the truth and the life. No one comes to the Father except through me'" (John 14:6).

God loves His people and does not want to see them perish. He offers the gift of eternal life to anyone willing to accept it. To receive this gift and begin a relationship with Him, we must confess that we are sinners, believe that Jesus' death on the cross paid the price for our sins, and humbly receive God's offer of eternal life through Christ.

> *"If we confess our sins, he is faithful and just and will forgive us our sins and purify us from all unrighteousness" (1 John 1:9).*

> *"If you declare with your mouth, 'Jesus is Lord,' and believe in your heart that God raised him from the dead, you will be saved" (Rom. 10:9).*

If you would like to accept God's gift of eternal life through Jesus Christ, pray the following prayer:

> **Dear God,**

> **I confess that I am a sinner. I believe Jesus died for my sins, and I want to accept your gift of eternal life. Thank you for forgiving me of my sins and for giving me a new life. I choose to begin living my life for you today.**
> **Amen**

If you prayed this prayer, tell a pastor or a Christian friend. If you don't already attend one, find a local church or Bible study where you can grow in your new life in Christ by studying God's word, enjoying Christian fellowship, and finding the guidance you need to begin living victoriously in Christ!

Leader Guide

If you choose to teach *Solomon Says* in a group setting, the following questions will help you organize class discussion. For each chapter, you will find a prayer focus, introductory question and questions that cover key points.

At the top of each chapter in the study, you'll notice a key verse that encapsulates the topic from Proverbs for that session. Participants are encouraged to memorize these key verses. For the verse recitation, consider having participants turn to a friend to say the verse rather than going around the room one at a time. This helps save class time and will relieve any anxiety for those who aren't comfortable speaking in front of a group.

Solomon Says is a study about wisdom, so allow plenty of time for discussion about people's experiences and how they have glorified God or learned a lesson through their experiences. We walk this road together, and God often uses us to speak to each other.

Introduction

Pray for open hearts to accept God's wisdom and allow the Holy Spirit to transform us through this study of Proverbs.

Introductory question: What is your name and one decision you had to make today or will have to make later in the day?

Discussion questions:

1. What do you know about the book of Proverbs? Discuss the type of Bible book, key theme, authors, date written and literary structure. A study Bible or Bible reference book will help with this question.
2. Read Proverbs 2:1-5. How do we find the knowledge of God? Do we listen for wisdom, cry aloud for it or search for it as for hidden treasure? If the answer is no, why don't we?
3. How can we make sure we base our daily decisions on God's wisdom?

Chapter 1: Humility

Pray for humble hearts and the ability to see areas where pride resides in our lives.

Introductory question: What is something you rely on for everyday living?

Discussion questions:

1. Is there anything on earth that we can rely on completely? Read Psalm 102:25-27. What does this verse say we can rely on?
2. To rely on God we must be humble. What are some synonyms and antonyms of humility? Review the four points of humility on page 4. How do you define humility?
3. Among the four examples of humility provided by Moses, Hosea, Esther and Jesus, whose situation can you relate to most? Who have you seen in your life that exemplifies humility?
4. What are the results of pride according to the proverbs listed on page 7? What are some examples you have witnessed where pride caused these results?
5. Can you relate to one of the situations in which Joseph, King Belshazzar or Peter exhibited pride? What do these situations look like in our lives?
6. Discuss the following idea from David Guzik's commentary on John 13:9 including a quote from William Temple: "Sometimes we show a servant's heart by accepting the service of others for us. If we only serve, and refuse to be served, it can be a sign of deeply rooted and well-hidden pride. 'Man's humility does not begin with the giving of service; it begins with the readiness to receive it. For there can be much pride and condescension in our giving of service'" Temple.[1]

Chapter 2: Honesty

Pray for help to see places in our lives where we need to be more honest.

Introductory question: Do you like to shop, and why?

Discussion questions:

1. It's important to be a shrewd shopper because dishonest business practices are common. What are some fraudulent business practices in our culture today?
2. Why do you think people are especially dishonest when it comes to money? Could you relate to any of the examples on pages 11-12?
3. What do the following verses tell us about money: 1 Timothy 6:10, Ecclesiastes 5:10, Proverbs 22:1, and Proverbs 22:16?
4. Read 1 Timothy 6:17-19. Can God provide for us and is He enough?
5. Read Psalm 24:1. Who is the owner and who is the steward?
6. If we ever question the integrity of something we want to do, what does Matthew 7:12 encourage us to do?
7. Look at the different reasons for lying listed on page 13. Share an example of your experience with one of these reasons. Can any of these types of lies be justified?
8. Read Rahab's story in Joshua 2:1-7. How can you reconcile Rahab's lie with God's command that we not tell falsehoods?
9. Self-deception is the devil's greatest tool. What is the best way to avoid self-deception?
10. Looking at the proverbs listed on page 15, which consequences for dishonesty have you experienced? Which rewards for honesty have you experienced?

Chapter 3: Heart Attitudes

Pray for transformed hearts as we learn to clear out ungodly beliefs and negative attitudes and replace them with godly beliefs and positive attitudes.

Introductory question: Do you generally see life through a cup half full or a cup half empty?

Discussion questions:

1. Look at the list of attitudes on page 17. Make a mental note to yourself what your prevailing attitude is today. Read Matthew 13:19. What can be sown in our heart? How can this help us if we have more negative attitudes than positive ones during our day?
2. According to 2 Corinthians 9:7 and Ephesians 3:17, what else resides in our hearts?
3. What does Proverbs 4:23 tell us to do? What are practical ways we can accomplish this?
4. What does Proverbs 15:13 say is the result of a heart that is not happy (consider the word *happy* to be like the word *well*)? What does a crushed spirit look like?
5. Do negative attitudes have an effect on your physical health? What is an example of this?
6. Read Proverbs 18:14. Can you think of an example of someone who exemplifies this verse?
7. What do you think about the idea that our spiritual beliefs have a significant effect upon how well our souls are, especially during difficult times?
8. What is the difference between body, soul, and spirit? Based on the idea that the Hebrew word for heart, *leb*, means mind, will, and emotions, where does the heart fit between body, soul, and spirit?

Chapter 4: Generosity

Pray for insight on how we can be more generous with our materials, time, and emotions and for opportunities to show generosity.

Introductory question: What is a favorite gift you have been given?

Discussion questions:

1. Gifts are examples of generosity. What types of gifts were just mentioned - material or time?
2. How is generosity both a sacrifice and a joy for the giver?
3. Read Hebrews 13:16. What is the first phrase in this verse? Why does generosity not come easily for us?
4. What comes to mind when you hear the word *stingy*? According to Proverbs 11:24 and 28:22, what is the result of stinginess?
5. Read Proverbs 11:25 and 19:17. What are the benefits of generosity? What do the benefits of refreshment, blessing, and reward from the Lord look like?

6. How can we be generous with our time? Do you have a special memory of when someone made it a point to spend time with you?

7. How can we be generous with our emotions? How does Colossians 3:12 apply to generosity?

8. Review the stories of Dorcas (Acts 9:36-39), Philip (Acts 8:26-40) and the Good Samaritan (Luke 10:30-35). What do these examples look like in modern times?

Chapter 5: Time Management

Pray for sensitivity to God's will regarding how we spend our time.

Introductory question: What is your favorite part of the day?

Discussion questions:

1. Define time. Why is it important to us?

2. On page 28, what are the qualifications for wasted time? What are some examples of wasted time in your life?

3. Can anyone relate to overscheduling? What are some reasons we overschedule ourselves and can we find justification for those reasons in the Bible?

4. What do these verses say about time: Ecclesiastes 3:1-8,17; James 4:13-15; Proverbs 16:3; Philippians 3:13-14; and Proverbs 6:6-8?

5. What is the difference between busyness and industriousness?

6. Read Proverbs 26:13-16. Can you think of an example in your life that is similar to any of the sluggard's habits?

7. Define rest as God qualifies it in Genesis 2:2. Do you have times of rest built in to your daily routine?

8. Have you been in a season of life where you were lonely and did not know what to do with your time? How can we get motivated and keep ourselves from sinking into depression during the slow seasons of life?

Chapter 6: Anger

Pray for the ability to understand our emotions and those of people around us so that we might be more patient and understanding with each other.

Introductory question: What is one of your pet peeves?

Discussion questions:

1. What is anger? What are common ways people express anger?

2. Is anger a primary or secondary emotion? Explain.

3. Look at the situations on pages 34-35. What are the primary emotions underlying these situations? If you have been in a similar situation and handled it well, how did you do it?

4. According to Proverbs 29:11, what does it take to keep anger under control? What does this wisdom look like?

5. Emotional Intelligence is being aware of your own emotions and understanding the emotions of those around you. How can this help us manage anger in ourselves and from others?

6. Can you relate to one of the stories on page 37 (Cain, Ahab, Joseph's brothers, or the older brother of the prodigal son)? How could they have handled their situations better? Have you ever felt the same way as they did in a similar situation? How did you react?

7. What is righteous anger? Have you felt righteous anger or been the recipient of it?

8. Read Exodus 32:19-20. Was Moses' anger righteous, and did he display it in a God-honoring way, and why?

9. What is the antidote for anger according to 1 Peter 4:8 and Proverbs 10:12?

10. Read Psalm 103:8-10. How would life look if we treated others as God treats us according to this passage?

Chapter 7: Godly Speech

Pray for God to help us say only what is beneficial for building up others.

Introductory question: Do you speak, or have you ever studied, a second language, and which one?

Discussion questions:

1. Why is language important?

2. What does Luke 6:45 say about the origin of our words?

3. Make a list of types of negative speech. According to the proverbs listed on pages 42-43, what are some results of negative words? Share an example for one of these.

4. What can we do if we're around others who are speaking negatively? What are some practical ways to avoid negative speech?

5. Make a list of types of positive speech and their results, based on Proverbs 10:11, 10:20-21, 12:6, and 15:4. What are ways we can learn to speak more positively?

6. Read Proverbs 13:3. What is an example of living this principle?

7. What can we do when we "put our foot in our mouth?"

8. What do Proverbs 10:19 and James 1:19 emphasize regarding our speech? How does pride cause us to not be a good listener?

9. Optional: Ask if anyone would like to share their testimony. Or, you might want to collect everyone's written testimonies to make a special booklet for the class.

Chapter 8: Discipline

Pray for God's help to receive discipline graciously and for courage and godly motives to administer discipline.

Introductory question: What is a rule your family had when you were growing up, or a rule your family has now?

Discussion questions:

1. Why are rules important?
2. Read Proverbs 3:11-12. What is discipline? How are we to view discipline and why does the Lord discipline us?
3. Have you had to administer discipline? If so, did your view of discipline change after that?
4. Have you experienced any of the benefits of discipline listed on page 52? Provide an example.
5. What are the right reasons for discipline and what are some wrong reasons for it? According to Hosea 2:15, what was the Lord's purpose for discipline?
6. According to Proverbs 22:6, why should parents discipline their children? What is at stake if children are not disciplined (see Proverbs 23:13-14)? Give an example of when you have seen the reward of a disciplined child and the consequence of an undisciplined one.
7. What do these verses say about disciplining spouses, friends, employees and coworkers: Proverbs 27:9, 17; Proverbs 28:23; and Hebrews 12:11? What is the ultimate reason for disciplining another person?

Chapter 9: Justice

Pray for restraint in judging others and doling out justice, and for the supernatural ability to forgive.

Introductory question: What is your favorite TV police/court/detective show?

Discussion questions:

1. What makes police/court/detective shows appealing?
2. Justice is the idea of protecting rights and punishing wrongs; it is a system of fairness and lawfulness. According to our key verse. Proverbs 20:22, who should serve justice?
3. Have you ever appointed yourself the judge to dole out punishment when you've been hurt by someone? Why is this way of thinking wrong according to Proverbs 24:12 and Matthew 7:1-2?
4. What does Matthew 5:44-45 tell us about how we should treat our enemies? Share an example of an adverse situation in which you loved an enemy and it turned out for the good.
5. Review the definition of *forgive* on page 65. What are some examples of offenses, flaws, and mistakes?
6. What do Proverbs 10:12 and 19:11 recommend we do with our anger toward another person?
7. How does Matthew 18:23-35 encourage us to be forgiving?
8. What are the benefits of forgiveness according to the following verses: Proverbs 19:11; Proverbs 10:12; Proverbs 25:21-22; Matthew 5:9, 44-45; Luke 6:37; and James 3:18?

9. What are the consequences of unforgiveness according to Proverbs 10:12, 17:9, and Matthew 6:15?

10. How does Matthew 18:35 say we are to forgive? How can we begin to heal when we have deep hurts?

Chapter 10: Marriage

Pray for wisdom and conviction for the married and single people in your class regarding marriage.

Introductory question: Do you or did you have a list of qualities you wanted in a mate and, if so, what was one of those qualities?

Discussion questions:

For Married Couples:

1. Respond to this Martin Luther quote: "Let the wife make the husband glad to come home, and let him make her sorry to see him leave."
2. Statistics show that nearly half of all marriages admit unfaithfulness, either physically or emotionally. Why do you think this occurs?
3. Define adultery. What are the consequences of adultery according to Proverbs 6:26, 31-35?
4. Read Proverbs 5:15-20. What is Solomon's advice to avoid adultery? What are practical ways you can implement Solomon's advice in your own marriage?
5. Solomon's counsel also applies to all of us, as the brides of Christ. How can we protect our relationship with the Lord, so that we do not stray from Him?

For Singles:

1. According to Proverbs 12:4, how is a wife of noble character described? What does the disgraceful wife do to her husband? How does Matthew 12:25 apply to the disgraceful wife's actions? Can you think of an example of either of these situations in a couple you know?
2. Marriage is not a quick decision to be taken lightly. It is life-altering and meant to be "till death do you part," so it is important to resolve to marry wisely. There are five non-negotiable qualities a Christian should look for in a mate listed on pages 74-75. Do you agree with this list? Would you add anything to the list?
3. Define the non-negotiable qualities and provide an example of what they look like in real life.
4. Do you need to grow in any of these qualities? Which ones?

---

1. William Temple quoted in "John 13-Jesus the Loving Servant," Enduring Word: David Guzik's Bible Commentary, accessed March 12, 2018, https://enduringword.com/bible-commentary/john-13.

ABOUT KHARIS PUBLISHING

Kharis Publishing is an independent publishing house with a core mission to publish impactful books, and channel proceeds into establishing mini-libraries or resource centers for orphanages in developing countries, so these kids will learn to read, dream, and grow. Every time you purchase a book from Kharis Publishing or partner as an author, you are helping give these kids an amazing opportunity to read, dream, and grow. Kharis Publishing is an imprint of Kharis Media LLC. Learn more at **https://kharispublishing.com/**.

CPSIA information can be obtained
at www.ICGtesting.com
Printed in the USA
LVHW100816040820
662298LV00010B/335